Gra Photography

JAMES RENNER is the author of *The Serial Killer's Apprentice* and several other works of nonfiction. His true-crime stories have appeared in *The Best American Crime Writing*, as well as the *Cleveland Scene* and Cracked.com. His method of using social media to solve cold cases was the subject of a CNN profile, in 2015. He has also written two novels, *The Man from Primrose Lane* and *The Great Forgetting*. He lives in Akron with his wife and children.

ALSO BY JAMES RENNER

NONFICTION

Amy: My Search for Her Killer

The Serial Killer's Apprentice

It Came from Ohio . . .

FICTION

The Man from Primrose Lane

The Great Forgetting

TRUE CRIME ADDICT

How I Lost Myself in the
Mysterious Disappearance of Maura Murray

JAMES RENNER

PICADOR
A THOMAS DUNNE BOOK
ST. MARTIN'S PRESS
NEW YORK

TRUE CRIME ADDICT. Copyright © 2016 by James Renner. All rights reserved.
Printed in the United States of America. For information, address Picador,
175 Fifth Avenue, New York, N.Y. 10010.

picadorusa.com • picadorbookroom.tumblr.com
twitter.com/picadorusa • facebook.com/picadorusa

Picador® is a U.S. registered trademark and is used by Macmillan Publishing Group,
LLC, under license from Pan Books Limited.

For book club information, please visit facebook.com/picadorbookclub or e-mail
marketing@picadorusa.com.

Designed by Omar Chapa

The Library of Congress has cataloged the Thomas Dunne Books edition as follows:

Names: Renner, james, 1978– author.
Title: True crime addict: how I lost myself in the mysterious disappearance of Maura
     Murray / James Renner.
Description: First edition. | New York : Thomas Dunne Books, 2016.
Identifiers: LCCN 2015049511 | ISBN 9781250089014 (hardcover) | ISBN
     9781250089021 (e-book)
Subjects: LCSH: Renner, James, 1978– | Murray, Maura, 1982– | Journalists—
     United States—Psychology—Case studies. | Missing persons—United States—
     Case studies. | Criminal investigation—United States—Case studies. | BISAC:
     TRUE CRIME / General. | BIOGRAPHY & AUTOBIOGRAPHY / Personal
     Memoirs.
Classification: LCC HV6762. U5 R45 2016 | DDC 363.2'336—dc23
LC record available at http://lccn.loc.gov/2015049511

Picador Paperback ISBN 978-1-250-11381-8

Our books may be purchased in bulk for promotional, educational, or business
use. Please contact your local bookseller or the Macmillan Corporate and
Premium Sales Department at 1-800-221-7945, extension 5442, or by e-mail
at MacmillanSpecialMarkets@macmillan.com.

First published by Thomas Dunne Books, an imprint of St. Martin's Press

First Picador Edition: June 2017

D   10 9 8 7 6 5 4

FOR KEITH

CONTENTS

Contents

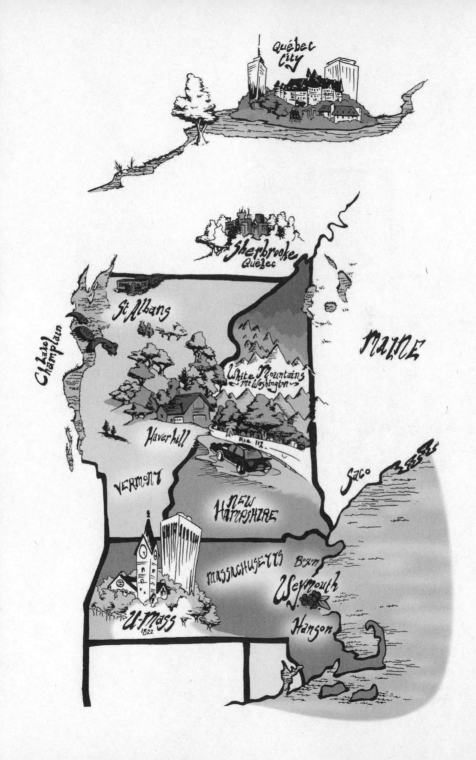

Truth is so rare that it is delightful to tell it.

—EMILY DICKINSON

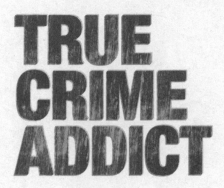

TRUE CRIME ADDICT

PROLOGUE

Butch Atwood almost made it home. It was dark on the Wild Ammonoosuc, but the lights of Atwood's school bus pushed back the night and reflected off the walls of snow gathered on either side of the two-lane blacktop. It had been a long day, carting kids to the ski slopes in Conway. Almost over.

Around the last curve, he spotted a car stuck in the snowbank on his side of the road, pointing back the way he'd come. It was a tight curve, nearly 90 degrees. The people who lived along this stretch were used to crashes in the night, especially in winter, when the pavement buckles with frost heaves. Butch slowed, stopped.

It was a dark Saturn. The front window was cracked, air bags blown, no flashers. Massachusetts plates. A pretty young woman with dark hair was standing outside. She looked about twenty years old. She was shivering.

"You okay?" he asked. Butch was a big fellow, 350 pounds. Rough-looking, with a stained, blond handlebar mustache.

"I'm just shook up," she said.

"I'll call the police for you," said Butch.

"No," the young woman replied. "Please don't. I already called Triple-A. They're sending a tow truck."

He knew she was lying. Cell phones don't work on the mountain, not that far up. He offered her a ride to his house, next door. She declined, so he left her beside the car and drove the last hundred feet to his cabin. He parked the bus beside his garage so he could watch the young woman from his driveway. Then he went inside, asked his wife to report the accident, and returned to his vehicle to fill out the day's paperwork for First School, the outfit he worked for.

Seven minutes later, the police arrived. By then, the young woman had vanished.

It was 7:45 P.M., February 9, 2004.

It was the last moment of peace for Butch Atwood.

ONE

The Girl with the Dragon Tattoo

The day my lawsuit against my former newspaper was settled, I drove out to the Lodge, the nudie bar on State Route 14. This was in 2009. For the last six years I had worked as a reporter. Not the sort of reporter you see in movies. I wasn't a beat reporter for some important daily paper. I wrote for the alt-weeklies, those free papers you find in bars and record stores and comic shops. There were two in Northeast Ohio, *The Free Times* and *Cleveland Scene,* before they merged in 2008. When I started out, a feature story paid $2,500. When I was fired six years later, the same story paid $300. Desperate times for a gonzo journalist.

The Lodge is tucked into the woods off SR 14, in Edinburg, a sleepy little hamlet south of Kent. Edinburg is 24.5 square miles of farmland, slanted fields of corn and soy, hog wallows, and mink farms. There's one traffic light in the school district. I fell in love with my wife out there when we played suspects in a high school production of *Rehearsal for Murder.* If you wanted to go on a date, there was the Dairy Queen. Otherwise, you had to drive twenty minutes into Ravenna. The Lodge didn't open until I was in college, and when it did it divided the town into sinners and saviors, and there was a public vote. In the end, the owner got the zoning variance he needed and the girls set up shop in the old honky-tonk across from the trailer yard. My best friend got drunk there one night and drove himself into the side of a house on his way home. I hadn't been there in a while.

For a tittie bar, the Lodge was kind of a nice place: a big cabin with soft leather couches, the head of a ten-point buck mounted over the fireplace. Against the back wall was a single pole in front of a black velvet curtain. I walked to the bar and ordered a Miller Lite in a bottle.

It's not like I go to strip clubs often. Maybe ten times in my life, mostly for bachelor parties. I'd paid three women to spank my buddy onstage the day he turned twenty-one. I wasn't ashamed to be there. I like how strip clubs smell. Like jolly ranchers and scotch.

"Want a dance?"

I turned to find a young blonde standing beside me. She was dressed in red, lacy lingerie. Her taut skin, covered in glitter, shimmered in the sparse light.

"No thank you," I said.

I have a thing for brunettes. And I don't like skinny. Not even athletic, really. I don't usually even buy a lap dance.

This happened a couple more times, that casual proposition. They all had silly names like Desiree, Sammi-with-an-I, or Eden. Really I thought I'd just sit at the bar for a couple drinks and watch the stage.

"I'm Gracie." This woman wore a thin black dress that stretched past her knees. Dark hair. Her body was soft and it curved in a nice way. Not busty, but healthy. I noticed right away that her eyes were different. She wasn't hustling, not like the other women. Or, if she was, she was better at it.

I bought her a drink. Vodka and grapefruit, if I remember right. And we talked for a bit. She was from West Virginia, liked to read. At the time, I was working my way through Stieg Larsson's *The Girl with the Dragon Tattoo*. This was before Larsson's thriller became a publishing phenomenon. Nobody I knew had read it yet. The only reason I even had a copy was my wife bought it for my birthday. Of course, when I browsed the jacket, I was immediately drawn to the similarities between my current predicament and the story—it begins, after all, with a journalist losing his job over a political exposé.

Gracie walked me to the "Champagne Room" and sat me down on a leather couch. It was a private nook with a door that she could close. A bouncer brought me another beer and left us alone. When the next song started, she danced for me. The dress came off. She wore a pair of black panties underneath. She climbed onto my lap and pressed her breasts against my face.

"Do you want to see my tattoo?"

"Sure," I said.

She stood and, gyrating to the music, turned around. The bottom half of her back was covered by a beautiful, inky-black dragon.

"Do you like it?"

I am no longer surprised by the weird coincidences that occur in my life. After writing about crime for some years, I came to believe that there was a kind of blueprint to the universe, a certain order to the shape of things. "Fearful symmetry," I've called it. Not necessarily intelligent design; more like a natural framework or something. I knew a cop once who'd investigated the case of a murdered girl. Found her body on County Road 1181, in Ashland

County. At the time, his cruiser number was 1181. Stuff like that. Stuff like this girl with the dragon tattoo.

Gracie took off her panties, turned around, and straddled my leg. She leaned her head back against my shoulder. We were waiting for another song to start.

"What do you do?" she asked.

"I don't know," I said. "I used to be a reporter. I wrote about crime. Unsolved murders, mostly. I got fired. I'm trying to figure out what to do next."

Something inside her changed. I got the feeling then that the woman sitting on my lap was no longer Gracie. I got the feeling she had somehow become more genuine.

When the music started again, she didn't move.

"You okay?" I asked.

She nodded against my neck. "My name's Jennifer," she said. "I'm not supposed to tell you my real name. But my real name is Jennifer."*

"Okay."

"I can dance for you. Or we could talk. Do you want to talk?"

"Do *you* want to talk?"

"Yes."

"Okay. What do you want to talk about?"

She didn't say anything for a beat. She slipped off my lap and dressed. Then she sat beside me, her legs kicked up over my lap, as if we were in a living room and she was waiting for a foot rub. "My sister was murdered," she said.

How do you respond to that? "Did they catch . . . him?" I asked, finally. "Her murderer?"

---

* Not her real name.

"Yes. Not for a while. But they just did. I spoke to the police down home. I'll have to go back to testify."

For the next half hour we sat in the Champagne Room and talked about the particulars of her sister's case. I gave her some advice on how to speak to the prosecutor and how to testify at trial. Then she hugged me and we just listened to the music.

This was a sign. Had to be, right? I was a journalist. Still. A crime writer. The universe wanted me to be. That's what Jennifer was about, I thought. Just because I didn't work for a newspaper, that didn't mean I had to stop.

TWO

Paramour

One day, while I was scanning Web sites about unsolved crimes at a neighborhood coffee shop called the Nervous Dog, the barista sat next to me and said in a whisper, "I have something important to tell you."

She was a country-cute eighteen-year-old with dark hair and a round face. The shop was nearly empty. Just me and one other customer.

"You're that reporter, the one that got fired for that article about Kevin Coughlin, right?"

I cringed. "That would be me, yes."

She seemed distressed. "I see you come in all the time but I didn't put it together that, you know, you were the reporter until I read about it in the paper." Had I offended her in some way I didn't understand? Was she Coughlin's cousin or something?

"It was me," she said. "I was your secret source."

That's how it started: an anonymous e-mail sent to my in-box at *Cleveland Scene* in the fall of 2008. The source claimed that State Senator Kevin Coughlin was having an affair with one of his campaign staffers. The tip included the name of the mistress's roommate, which was enough for me to do some digging. I had always assumed the e-mail had come from someone in Columbus, a fellow congressman or political rival. I never expected the tip had come from a part-time coffee-slinger.

Coughlin was a Republican blowhard from Cuyahoga Falls, a blue-collar suburb of Akron often referred to as "Caucasian Falls." He was infamous in greater Akron for a failed coup against the local GOP leadership, led for twenty-five years by a shrewd man named Alex Arshinkoff. Not for nothing, but according to police reports, the married, publicly straight Arshinkoff once picked up a twenty-one-year-old hitchhiker downtown, rubbed his leg, and asked the young man if he "wanted to make some money" before the guy managed to escape by jumping out of the car. In 2008, Coughlin threw his hat into the governor's race.

After the tip came in I researched Coughlin's background and quickly got a sense of his character. He and fifty other members of the Ohio House of Representatives had voted to exempt themselves from public records laws. Coughlin sponsored a bill that would have allowed patients to be treated by a physical therapist without a prescription or referral from their primary physician. His wife was a practicing physical therapist. He asked for campaign contributions from Time Warner while sitting on the Senate committee that wrote regulatory policy for cable companies. You get the picture.

The first thing I did was track down the people who rented the apartment across the hall from where Coughlin's alleged mistress lived. The residents confirmed that the congressman came by when the young woman was home, alone. His SUV, with personalized plates, would be parked out front late into the night. Then I located the roommate, who went into explicit detail about how Coughlin would come over to have loud sex with his staffer in her thin-walled bedroom while the roommate sat in the living room watching TV. When Coughlin caught wind of my reporting, he went ballistic.

One night he left a message on *Scene* publisher Matt Fabyan's phone, blaming Arshinkoff for the leak. "He's been peddling this story ever since he hit on me," he said. The next day, we got the first letter from Coughlin's attorney, demanding we kill the story. But word had traveled and other sources were contacting me.

A former Coughlin full-time staffer, a guy named Mike Chadsey, was the one who gave me the info about how the congressman would take his mistress to Ohio State football games and pay for the trips with campaign money. They had a routine: Chadsey and Coughlin's paramour would meet the congressman in the parking lot of the Sheraton Hotel in Cuyahoga Falls, ride with Coughlin to Columbus, then return to the hotel. Campaign reports show that Coughlin paid for rooms at the Sheraton, billing it as: "Staff Accommodations."

When the newspaper bigwigs back in Scranton got wind of the letter from Coughlin's attorney, they spiked my story and told me to work on something else. The paper could not risk a lawsuit, said CEO Matt Haggerty. I told him that if he couldn't risk a lawsuit, he couldn't run a newspaper. He told me I was fired. I told him to go fuck himself. Then I e-mailed the article to every contact in my Rolodex. The story was picked up and reprinted online, circulated throughout the statehouse in Columbus. *Slate* picked up the Jerry Maguire-ish mission statement I sent to the employees of *Scene* on my way out.

It got messy. I sued Haggerty, *Scene,* and Coughlin for wrongful termination. The *Akron Beacon Journal* and *The Columbus Dispatch* covered the details of the court filings. Eventually, Coughlin, through his lawyer, admitted he never had cause to sue the paper, that his threats to my editor and publisher were baseless. Haggerty and I came to an agreement on the rest.

The young barista happened upon her intel through a local painter, who was the father of the mistress's roommate. Here's how small Akron is: That roommate's father painted my house, which I had purchased from the barista's uncle. Wrap your head around that. I looked at the young woman sitting across from me at the Nervous Dog and said, "Thank you."

THREE

Full Disclosure

"I'm thinking of writing about crime again," I said.

My psychologist smiled, tightly. Roberta was a seasoned counselor working out of a square office below a fitness center in West Akron. I'd been seeing her for three years. I picked her out of the yellow pages in 2006, around the time my first book was published. It was a nonfiction account of my investigation into the abduction and murder of a ten-year-old girl named Amy Mihaljevic. After the book was released, I started having panic attacks in grocery stores. My mind kept insisting that the guy in front of me at checkout was keeping girls tied up in his basement. Turns out I had contracted secondhand post-traumatic stress disorder, the kind embedded war journos sometimes get. That was an idea that took me a long time to accept, by the way, and I still feel guilt when thinking about it. After all, I never served in a war. What the hell do I have to complain about that's so terrible? And yet, there was no denying the symptoms. A daily Cymbalta took the edge off. Roberta and I met every other week for an hour and she listened to me talk about my fears. I liked her. She was wise from experience. Years ago, she had been the hired counselor for a very famous band, traveling with the musicians on tour, keeping them sane and mostly sober.

"You think that's a good idea?" she asked. "Writing about crime again?"

"I need something to focus on," I said. "I need to find a way to make money. And it's something I know how to do."

It was a great plan, I thought. I could work on the new book after my wife got home at three—she taught high school choir a couple towns away. I'd watch our kid in the morning and write at night.

"I have the results from your MMPI test," she said, moving on.

That would be the Minnesota Multiphasic Personality Inventory test, a psychological exam developed by a couple of shrinks in 1939 at the University of Minnesota. It's the litmus test for psychopathy they use to this day. The CIA gives it to candidates to suss out potential mental health issues in their operatives. The test is a list of 504 simple statements. You fill in bubbles to denote how strongly you "agree" or "disagree" with each statement. Two examples: "I am very seldom troubled by constipation" and "I like to read newspaper articles on crime." I was taking it now because we were considering an end to our counseling sessions and Roberta wanted to see where my head was.

"How'd I do?" I asked.

"Your results were very similar to those of Ted Bundy, the serial killer."

That's one of those statements you just can't unhear.

"Don't get too upset," said Roberta. "You may have the psychopathy of a dangerous man, but so do many cops. In fact, a lot of

CEOs would have scored the same as you, or worse. Donald Trump is probably a sociopath. But it's what makes him successful."

"How'd I do on the intelligence test?" I asked. She'd given me a second test the last time we'd met—a long series of logic puzzles.

"Perfect score. And that's the good news. You have the intelligence to temper your psychopathy. You're smart enough to be aware of your own compulsions, to find healthy outlets for your anger before you explode. You're smart enough to keep yourself safe."

My heart was beating fast. It felt like I had just been diagnosed with cancer. One of the bad kinds that never go away. I'd come here seeking a solution and she'd just told me my problem was incurable.

"You will learn to live with it," she said. "You just have to."

"What about the crime writing?" I asked.

She thought for a moment and then said, "I think it's a good idea. Use it to channel that dark side. Your mind works like the people you chase after. Like a good detective. You're a sociopath, too."

I left Roberta's office feeling kind of numb. Driving home, I thought about what makes someone dangerous. Was it genetics? There was a case to be made there, I knew. But I pushed that line of thinking aside—I wasn't ready to go there yet. Could a child's environment make them good or bad? Were environmental factors, alone, enough to push a kid one way or another? My stepmother used to punch me. Was that why I needed to be medicated as an adult? I had fallen in love with Amy Mihaljevic when I saw her MISSING poster hanging on a utility pole when I was eleven years old. What was that all about?

What I did was I went home and I hugged my son.

How much of me is in Casey? I wondered.

After he fell asleep I got to thinking about writing again. I wanted a big case. Nothing local. Something difficult. I remembered this episode of *20/20* I'd seen recently. It was a special report on two missing women. Brooke Wilberger and Maura Murray were college students who excelled in school and then vanished within a few months of each other, in 2004. Brooke's case immediately struck me as an abduction. She'd been cleaning lampposts (helping her sister, who was a property manager) in the parking lot of an apartment complex in the Oregon town of Corvallis but never showed up for her lunch break. Her car was still in the lot and she'd left her car keys, purse, and flip-flops behind.

Maura's case was more baffling. A nursing student from UMass, about to be engaged. Vanished in the North Country after crashing into a snowbank. Police found no signs of foul play, no footprints leading into the woods. She simply disappeared before police arrived on the scene seven minutes after the accident. It didn't feel like an abduction to me. But nobody knew where she was. And there was a second mystery wrapped around Maura's disappearance like a serpent coiled around a pepper tree: What the hell was Maura doing in New Hampshire in the first place?

FOUR

All-American Girl

The first thing you learn as a reporter is that nothing you read in the newspaper is true. Truth in reporting is a lie. Here's how it really works: A reporter is assigned to gather facts on an event—let's say it's a crash involving two cars at the intersection of Main and State. The person driving Car A will have a different story to tell than the driver of Car B. And those stories will differ, sometimes greatly, with the statements of witnesses on the sidewalk. But what really happened? I mean, there must be an inherent truth, right? Maybe. But the reporter should never assume he knows which version is most accurate. The best a good reporter can do is gather all the information and present every side of the story. And you know what? Even then, the article will be junk. Because, invariably, a name will be spelled wrong or some little detail will be misinterpreted. The crash will be reported as happening at the intersection of Main and County or some shit. Or the writer will refer to one of the cars as a Saturn when it was really a Vibe. Every article you've ever read is a little untrue. I guarantee it.

And still, you don't go trying to solve a cold case without first reading everything that has already been written about it, even if you know it's a bunch of bunk.

I began my research into the disappearance of Maura Murray that fall of 2009, combing through old newspaper articles for the names of sources and avenues of investigation, mindful that some of what I was reading was incorrect. And slowly, a portrait of Maura Murray emerged.

Everyone agrees that Maura was beautiful and we can accept at least that much as truth. Family photographs show a bright-faced young woman with dark brown shoulder-length hair, which she often wore in a tight ponytail. Apple cheeks and crazy dimples. A button nose. Skinny from running. A hundred and twenty pounds, soaking wet.

Maura was from Hanson, Mass, a quiet town between Boston and the Cape. Too small for its own public high school, it shares one with Whitman, the town next door. Hanson is old by American standards, settled in 1632. It's where Ocean Spray started harvesting cranberries. Hanson is lousy with cranberry bogs and swamps and thin tributaries reaching for the ocean. Random trivia: Rocky Marciano once owned a house on Main Street.

Born on May 4, 1982, Maura was the fourth of five children. Her father, Fred, was a nuclear medicine tech; her mother, Laurie, was a nurse. She had an older brother, Freddie, Jr.; two older sisters, Kathleen and Julie; and a little brother, Kurt. Maura liked to hike. Sometimes Fred took her camping in the White Mountains, on the sides of the great peaks with presidential names, just across the border into New Hampshire. At first glance, the Murrays appeared to be the quintessential Irish-American family—lots of kids and love to spare.

In high school, Maura excelled in athletics and academics. She was point guard on the varsity basketball team as a freshman and built a legacy in track and cross-country. Talk to someone who lived in Hanson at that time and they'll tell you how they remember seeing her running, always running, from one side of town to the other. She was the school's star runner, and graduated fourth in her class. She was as comfortable in track gear as she was in a prom dress. She scored a 1420 on the SATs.

After high school, Maura was accepted into West Point, following Julie to the prestigious military academy. She met her boyfriend, William Rausch, there. He was intelligent, but also a hunk—picture a Paul Walker type. They were a power couple. Maura spent three semesters studying chemical engineering at West Point before transferring to UMass, where she enrolled in the nursing program, earning solid marks. Billy, a year older, graduated from the academy and was stationed in Fort Sill in Lawton, Oklahoma, at the time of Maura's disappearance. The papers said he was going to propose. For their honeymoon, they planned to stay in the White Mountains. At UMass, Maura worked two jobs in addition to doing her nursing clinicals: dorm security and as a part-time guard for the campus art gallery.

Billy's mother, Sharon, was interviewed for a four-part article titled "All-American Girl" that was posted on the missing-persons Web site, ProjectJason.org. "Smiling and quiet laughter are as natural to Maura as breathing," she told the reporter. "Thank you notes from Maura were received by anyone who offered to her the slightest kindness. Maura's favorite color is blue. She likes fruit and French-Vanilla Coffee for breakfast. She appreciates simple things like Gala or Fuji Apples or a 'just ripe banana.' A large salad with all of the fixings is Maura's choice for lunch or dinner each day."

In the summers, Maura stayed with Billy's family in rural Ohio. Sharon recalled one time when Maura leaned over to her husband and said softly, in her New England accent, "I see you have a sitting mower. I have always wanted to ride a sitting mower." Billy's dad taught her how to work the tractor and she spent hours buzzing around the property, clipping grass in the feral fields that bordered the yard.

In the early dispatches during the weeks following Maura's disappearance, nobody had an unkind word to say about the missing woman. The image they painted of Maura in the press was that of an angelic innocent, a diligent, hardworking young woman. No enemies in the world. Perfect to a fault.

But that perfectly painted image doesn't hold up when we consider Maura's actions and behavior in the four days leading up to her disappearance.

FIVE

Past Is Prologue

It was late Thursday, the fifth of February, 2004, and Maura was a few hours into her shift at the security desk in Melville Hall, a freshman dormitory on the UMass campus named for the guy who wrote the ultimate book on pointless obsession. Around ten o'clock, Maura got a call from her sister Kathleen on her cell phone. When Maura's supervisor checked in on her around 1 A.M., she found Maura nearly catatonic. Something had deeply upset her, but Maura didn't want to talk about it. All she could say was, "My sister." The supervisor escorted her back to Kennedy Hall, where Maura lived.

On Saturday morning, Maura's father arrived in Amherst. According to early reports Fred was helping her find a new car. Maura's '96 Saturn was on its last legs. At the end of the day, Fred treated Maura and a friend of hers to dinner and drinks at a local brewpub. Then Maura dropped Fred off at his motel and returned to campus in his car to attend a late-night party.

At 3:30 A.M., as she was traveling back to her father's motel, Maura crashed Fred's car into a guardrail. Police arrived at the scene. The tow truck driver gave Maura a ride to where her father was staying, and she slept in Fred's room that night.

The next morning, Maura helped her father find a rental so that he could get to his job on Monday. At the time, Fred was working at a hospital in Bridgeport, Connecticut, about two hours away, and living out of the Homestead Suites there.

Maura used her personal computer on Monday to MapQuest directions to Stowe, Vermont. She searched for rental properties in the White Mountains area. Then she e-mailed professors and her boss at the art gallery, explaining that she would be gone for a week due to a "death in the family." At 3:40 P.M. Maura withdrew $280 from a local ATM, essentially emptying her bank account. She was next seen at a neighborhood liquor store buying a significant amount of alcohol.

Three and a half hours later, Maura crashed her Saturn into a snowbank on Wild Ammonoosuc Road in Haverhill, New Hampshire.

Police who responded to the scene of the accident did not find any footprints leading into the woods. The car was locked, but an open box of wine could be seen inside and red liquid had stained the upholstery. The air bags had been deployed and the windshield was cracked on the driver's side. By all appearances, it looked like a driver trying to escape a DUI, not an uncommon event. The cop assumed the driver would show up at the impound lot later, with a hangover, asking for his or her car back.

The Saturn was towed away.

Police attempted to contact Fred, the registered owner of the Saturn, the next day; by then, after speaking to Butch, they had realized the driver was probably his daughter, Maura Murray. At

12:36 P.M. they issued a BOLO—police-speak for Be on the Lookout—for women matching Maura's description. The only number they had for Fred was for his home in Massachusetts. A message was left on his machine, explaining the developing situation in Haverhill. Kathleen would eventually get this message and phone her father as he was leaving work at five that afternoon.

Detectives learned Maura had lied to her professors on her way out of Amherst: There had been no death in the family. When investigators got into her dorm room, they found all her belongings packed neatly into boxes. She'd taken the posters off her walls. It appeared she had planned to leave UMass and never come back.

SIX

The Gatekeeper

By January of 2011, when I finally began my reporting, any urgency the police had once felt to find Maura Murray had died away. The ground searches had been suspended years ago. The media had lost interest, too. News of the case had faded to a trickle of information released through the official family Web site, MauraMurrayMissing.com. It's one of those low-rent make-your-own sites, easy to build in a hurry. Pictures of Maura smiling with friends. Links to news articles. There was an e-mail address for the site's administrator. I sent a message and a while later I heard back from a woman who first identified herself as Maura's aunt.

I preferred to speak to Fred Murray first. Maura's father had led the searches into the North Country woods in the weeks after she went missing. "Aunt" Helena Dwyer-Murray promised to pass along my messages. In the meantime, I interviewed her for some background on the case and where it stood presently. We spoke over the phone and she brought me up to speed.

Helena had never met Maura. Her late father-in-law and Fred's father were brothers. The connection had no blood, but somehow she'd become the Murrays' spokesperson. It happens. The families of the missing often need someone a little removed from the trauma to take the lead. Grief cuts sharper the closer you get to the victim.

I had a lot of questions about Butch Atwood, the bus driver who was the last person to speak with Maura. If he was really concerned about her, why did he leave the scene of the accident? Could he have taken her? I had interviewed enough detectives to know that, statistically, the last person to see a missing woman is usually the best suspect.

Atwood was on the family's list of suspects, Helena said. She told me that Atwood moved to Florida not long after Maura disappeared. A private investigator working for the Murrays interviewed him, but I would never get the chance. Atwood passed away in 2009.

Many of the key people involved in Maura's investigation had scattered to the wind by the time I got involved. The lead detective, John Scarinza, was retired. The chief of police in Haverhill, Jeff Williams, was no longer chief. Maura's mother, Laurie, had passed, too. She died on Maura's birthday, in 2009.

"And Fred? Depends on the day, really," said Helena. "Nobody really sees the true Fred. But it shines through on some of these TV programs, the pain he feels."

"Why was Maura in New Hampshire that night?" I asked. "What's the family think about that?"

"She was heading to Bartlett," she said, simply. "We think she was heading to Bartlett because that's where she had stayed before, with Fred. But then she got in that accident. The roads up there are bad in the winter. The frost heaves are terrible."

"What do you think she was doing?"

"I just think she was going away for a few days. I think she was upset and wanted a couple days off."

"What about suicide? Is that an option?"

"She had textbooks in the car with her. Tooth whitener. You don't take tooth whitener or birth control pills with you if you plan to commit suicide."

Helena told me that when police got a warrant to search the car, they found expensive jewelry inside: a watch and a pendant. But Maura's cell phone was missing. So was her backpack.

I asked about friends of Maura's who might know more. Helena mentioned two: Kate Markopoulos and Sara Alfieri. Both women were students at UMass in 2004. Both Kate and Sara had attended a party with Maura the weekend before she drove into New Hampshire. Then Helena said something odd.

"Sara told Fred her story, but she will not talk about it with anybody else."

"Why not?"

Helena would say nothing more about it, only that I shouldn't bother trying to contact Sara on my own. "She'll never talk to you."

Helena told me that Maura was not the only person who had vanished from that area of New Hampshire. In 2010, a forty-year-old man named Christopher Flynn disappeared not far from the scene of the accident. Flynn was from Massachusetts, too.

"Haverhill, this place, it's not a destination," Helena said. "So what was he doing up there?"

I heard back from Helena a couple weeks later. She called my cell as I was pulling into a car wash with my son—Casey loved

going through the monster car wash in Cuyahoga Falls. What
Helena said came as a surprise.

"I spoke to Fred," she said. "He does not want a book written
about this. And he doesn't want to talk to you."

SEVEN

Forget the Past

It was during this time that my son began to get violent.

At first we used the word "tantrum." *Oh, Casey's just having a tantrum. He'll calm down in a couple minutes.* He was only three, after all. Three-year-olds have tantrums.

When Casey got mad, he raged, he wanted to hurt. He wanted to hit and kick and bite. And it was little things that set him off. Transitions, mostly. Time to stop playing and take a bath. Time to go to bed.

We had Casey evaluated by child psychologists at Case Western Reserve University, in Cleveland. It was one of those places where a bunch of shrinks sit in one room and watch their subject through mirrored glass. My wife, Julie, and I stood with the doctors and watched Casey interact with a prompter. They gave him an intelligence test. When they were done, the lead doctor sat us down and explained that she thought Casey was "spectruming," or showing characteristics of autism.

Maybe I was in denial, but I didn't buy the diagnosis. My kid wasn't remote like Rain Man. Autistic people tend to lack empathy. But when Casey was happy he could be the most loving little guy. He liked to snuggle at the end of the day, watch *SpongeBob* with me. Whenever he left someplace, he had to hug everyone in the room. And everything he was doing, I recognized. This was how I had acted when I was his age.

With Casey, I found that if I kept him busy, his tantrums were less frequent. We went to the zoo a lot. Sometimes we walked down to the river and threw rocks in the water until he was good and dirty. If he didn't have something to focus his mind on, that's when he ran into trouble.

I got it. Thirty years down the road of life, I still grew easily frustrated and depressed if I wasn't on deadline. Without the rigid structure of newspaper reporting, I was becoming increasingly manic. The only thing keeping me sane, really, was the mystery of Maura Murray's disappearance.

I'm a bit of an unsolved-mysteries junkie. The colder the case, the better, as far as I'm concerned. I once flew to Seattle on my own dime for a sit-down with the FBI agent in charge of the D. B. Cooper case (America's only unsolved hijacking). I've spent years trying to bring Amy Mihaljevic's killer to justice. In 2006, I spent two months researching the disappearance of two girls from Cleveland's West Side: Amanda Berry and Gina DeJesus. I still wondered about them. I met with both the Berry and DeJesus families on that story. *Do everything you can to find our girls,* they said. In my experience, family members of the missing clamor for the attention of reporters. A simple statistic: The more media coverage a case gets, the better its odds of being solved.

Until Fred Murray, I had never heard of a parent of a missing person who turned down the chance for national exposure. I might have scuttled my plans for a book right there. Without co-operation from Maura's family, what did I have? But the story had its hooks in me. It was unlike any missing-persons case I'd ever read about because of its weird mystery-within-a-mystery. Maura did not vanish on a normal day. She had broken her routine; she'd driven into the North Country. What was she doing up there? Where was she going?

I've always had better luck getting a source to talk if I showed up at their home. If they can see me, see how bumbling and affable I can be, they usually end up talking, even if they've told me no over the phone. But everyone connected to Maura's case lived hundreds of miles away. Well, almost everyone. Maura's boyfriend, Billy Rausch, was from Marengo, Ohio, a workaday town between Mansfield and Columbus, a ninety-minute drive down Route 71 from my house.

So I went to Marengo and found Billy's childhood home, a ranch sitting on a small lot. I parked my car and walked around back, where a sliding glass door looked into a cluttered living room. Billy's mother, Sharon, appeared in a long robe.

Sharon has reddish hair and sharp features and comes across as highly intelligent. Her love for Maura was apparent in the news clips I'd seen on YouTube. She had cared for the young woman from Mass who'd stolen her son's heart, and had opened up her home to her.

"I'm James Renner," I said. "I'm writing the book about Maura?"

Sharon nodded. "I know," she said.

"Sorry to drop in like this, but would you have some time to talk about her?"

"Well, I'm a little under the weather right now," she said.

Now that she mentioned it, Sharon looked tired. Worn out. But not sick. Maura's disappearance had been seven years ago. Was she still carrying that tragedy around inside her, like a bad cold?

"Maybe when you're feeling better, you could call me and we could set up a time to meet."

"Sure," she said.

I left my number and my book on Amy Mihaljevic's case.

"I have to drive to New Hampshire," I said to my wife one night when we were lounging on the couch at the end of the day. Julie rolled her eyes at me.

"The anniversary of Maura's disappearance is next week," I said. "I want to be there to see who drives by the scene of the accident. For the book."

"I hate these stories. You always have to find some dead girl. It's so codependent."

"No one knows if she's dead," I said. "And she isn't a girl. She's grown up. There's no dead kids in this one."

"That you know of."

"So . . ."

"So, what?" said Julie. "If you have to go, go. But I won't be happy about it."

"Thank you."

"Just don't do anything dangerous. Or stupid."

A week later I was driving drunk down Wild Ammonoosuc Road, lost in its dark turns.

EIGHT

Last Shift at Melville

Karen Mayotte was the first person to notice that something was wrong with Maura Murray. Until I tracked Karen down through social media, she had never been interviewed about the night Maura broke down at work. We met up at Finders Pub in West Boylston, Massachusetts, two days before the seventh anniversary of Maura's disappearance.

The best word I can use to describe Karen is "bubbly." She's the sort of person who says things like "Holy moly" a lot. She's energetic like a kid but maternal at the same time. In fact, she has four children and was working as a first-grade teacher when we met. Back in 2004, Karen was the shift supervisor for the UMass residence hall security staff. At night, she patrolled the campus, checking to make sure doors were locked, alarms were set, and that each dorm had a security guard posted in the lobby. During the day, she studied the Holocaust and worked with Sudanese refugees.

Though I protested, she bought me a Sam Adams and some fried clams and I ate while she talked. I got the impression Karen was very happy that someone was finally listening, that she'd been waiting to share this story.

"Maura worked at Melville Hall," Karen explained. "She worked the security desk, checking IDs." Melville is located in the Southwest quadrant of UMass, an area with a reputation for being the craziest quad to work. When the Sox play, things can get out of hand down there. Underage drinking, drugs, vandalism.

At UMass, Maura was a bit of a loner, said Karen. Sometimes, she'd see Maura eating lunch alone. It was hard to get Maura to open up. When she saw Maura reading a book about hiking the White Mountains titled *Not Without Peril*, Karen told her that she'd been there as a kid. "I lied. I'd never been there. But I wanted to get her talking. She told me about her favorite trails around Mount Washington."

Karen checked in with her lead supervisor around 10:30 the night of Maura's breakdown. "He said, 'Something's up with Maura. Just so you know.' She had been crying. I went to see what was up."

When Karen arrived at Melville, Maura was staring into space. "I don't know how to explain it. She was just zoned out. No reaction at all. She was unresponsive."

Maura had a cell phone on the desk, which was against regulations, but Karen let it slide.

"I pretended to look at the write-in sheet and kind of watched her out of the corner of my eye," said Karen. "Then she said two words, 'My sister.' It was very uncomfortable. I watched two people come in. One was a boy. She didn't even ask for his ID. She was catatonic, I think. Sobbing slightly, and staring at the door."

Karen stepped outside and called her boss, Nathaniel Whitmer. She told him that Maura was in rough shape. Whitmer told Karen to send her home. So Karen packed up Maura's stuff. She signed her out in the log because Maura couldn't do it herself. They walked the short distance to Kennedy Hall together.

"I asked her if she wanted me to bring her some Dunkins," said Karen. But Maura didn't want donuts or coffee. "She said something about nursing in the morning. She wanted to go to sleep." Karen was so concerned, she suggested to Maura that she check herself into the hospital, get some mental help.

"I said, 'Maura, do you have someone to talk to?' She said, 'I have a roommate.'" That was a lie, Karen learned later. Maura's room was a single.

When they arrived at Kennedy, Karen hugged Maura and kissed her on the cheek. She watched Maura walk upstairs.

The next morning, there was a snowstorm and classes were canceled. "I thought, *That's cool for her. She can get some rest.*"

Four days later, Karen got a call from UMass police. They told her Maura was missing, that her car had been found abandoned in the White Mountains. Karen went to the police station and filled out a report. She never heard back from the detectives.

"I don't know what was wrong with her," said Karen. "Was she suicidal? Why else would she go up there?"

NINE

The Zoo

Three Indians—Umpanchla, Quonquont, and Chick-walopp—"sold" Amherst to a white guy, in 1658, for some wampum. The area is a picturesque slice of New England, nestled between the Connecticut River and Quabbin Reservoir, patches of wood full of hickory and black cherry and red oak. This bit of land inspired some of America's finest writers: Emily Dickinson, Robert Frost, Robert Francis. It wasn't called Amherst, though, until it was incorporated in 1759 and named for a famous (read: infamous) British officer of the French and Indian War. It was Jeffrey Amherst's idea to give smallpox-infected blankets to Chief Pontiac's army during the siege of Fort Pitt. The disease decimated the Indian tribe. Some have suggested renaming the town.

There are two institutions of higher learning here: Amherst College, a private liberal arts school with about 1,800 students, and UMass, the largest public university in New England, with around 27,000 enrolled each year. Should history ultimately regard Maura Murray's disappearance as nothing but a clever hoax, UMass may finally surpass Amherst College in hoodwinking chicanery. Until that time, the honor goes to the smaller school, which, to this day, is the curator of the corpse of the Feejee Mermaid, the skeleton of a half-fish/half-human monstrosity that toured with P. T. Barnum's circus. Visitors can see the remains at Amherst's art museum.

UMass, though. It isn't a campus—it's a goddamn city. The university's W.E.B. Du Bois Library, at twenty-six stories, is the second-tallest library in the world. Its sports teams compete with the best in the country and its departments roll out Fulbright Scholars like a nerd assembly line. Amherst pubs have launched the careers of crooners for The Pixies, Dinosaur Jr., and They Might Be Giants. But churning out this volume of students who find success comes with a dark side. ABC News once dubbed UMass the most violent campus in the country. The townies refer to it as ZooMass. Or, simply, the Zoo.

I arrived at the Zoo on February 8, and the campus was a cold, sleeping city of concrete, brick, and glass. I parked my car at a meter and made my way to a large, ugly structure that looked like some communist-era Moscow public works project, or maybe an outdated computer cartridge set on its side. The Murray D. Lincoln Campus Center is a hub for students and also a hotel. In the basement is a morgue. But not the kind for dead bodies. This morgue is for newspapers, specifically the bound archives of the Zoo's student paper, *The Daily Collegian*. I made my way downstairs, past a sign that read: FREE BRUINS T-SHIRT WITH BLOOD DONATION!

I found a faculty adviser who escorted me to a nook with a threadbare couch. The large hardback books of old newsprint were scattered atop the coffee table and the file cabinets that lined the wall. I dug around until I found the archives from the spring of 2004.

The first on-campus article about Maura's disappearance didn't appear until February 17. It ran under the headline: NURS-ING STUDENT MISSING FOR DAYS. Student reporters had spoken to the dean of nursing and put a time on that final e-mail from Maura. It was sent at 1:24 P.M. on February 9. The e-mail stated that she was heading home for the week due to "a death in the family."

The *Collegian* ran a lengthy update on the search for Maura the following semester, which included a brief interview with Laurie, Maura's mother. Older sister Kathleen was also interviewed, and the reporter asked about that disturbing phone call the night of Maura's breakdown: "It was just a phone call. It made no differ-ence to me," said Kathleen. "It was just Maura calling me. That was that. I told her about my day and quarreling with my fiancé. I don't know what I could have done to upset her. Seriously, I think she just wanted to get out of work."

I jotted down the names of the sources mentioned in the articles and then walked around campus a bit. The Zoo is quiet in the winter, but you can feel the mass of students packed inside the dorms, like great batteries of potential energy. I dropped by Melville. When Maura worked there, it was an all-female dorm. Just behind it was John F. Kennedy Tower, where Maura had lived, a bleak concrete rectangle, imposing.

I felt like a creep, hanging around the women's dorms, so I returned to the car and drove out to the liquor store where Maura had stopped on her way out of Amherst. The management had changed over the years. The new owners knew nothing about the disappearance. I bought some wine, a Coke, and a few sample bot-tles of Jameson Irish Whiskey, the kind they serve you on cross-country flights. I got some lunch, cruised around town, and waited until 4:30, about the latest Maura could have left Amherst the day she disappeared, according to the accepted time line. Then I drove for Haverhill, New Hampshire.

I re-created Maura's journey into the North Country. When I crossed the border into New Hampshire, I unscrewed the top of a Jameson bottle and emptied it into a half-can of Coke, started drinking, and began to look for the exit that would take me into Haverhill and the part of the Matrix that held Maura's secret.

TEN

Hacking the Universe

There's this theory that our universe is nothing but a computer simulation. The idea is that we all exist inside a mostly pointless video game programmed by some higher life-form. You might be surprised to learn that this is a very old idea. In his *Meditations on First Philosophy,* in 1641, René Descartes proposed that the observable world might be a great trick orchestrated by an "evil demon." And Descartes's argument was inspired by Plato's "Allegory of the Cave," written nearly twenty-five hundred years ago. Today, the notion of a giant computer simulation is very much in vogue in the world of theoretical physics. And here's the scary part: It looks like it really might be true.

Dr. Nick Bostrom, director of the Future of Humanity Institute at Oxford, explained to *The New York Times* in 2007 that soon, humanity will develop computers that are fast enough and big enough to run a simulation of the entire history of the universe, a copy of our own reality. They'll use it to study the cosmos, from the Big Bang to the Heat Death of Everything. Eventually, there will be thousands, millions of these simulated versions of reality.

Still with me? Good, 'cause here's where it gets weird. Supposing all this is possible (and tech geeks promise the computing power will be achieved by the middle of this century), then we would be stupid to assume that the reality in which we live is the "original" world that spawned the first simulations. Mathematically, it is far more probable that our world, too, is nothing but one of these computer programs. "My gut feeling," Bostrom told the *Times*, "and it's nothing more than that, is that there's a twenty percent chance we're living in a computer simulation."

One aspect our universe clearly shares with video games is the strange way quarks behave when they're not being watched. Quarks are the building blocks of the universe—the tiniest bits, the "pixels," of our reality. Scientists discovered some time ago that quarks exist as a probability wave until someone looks at them and they collapse into matter that can be quantified.

How does any of this relate to Maura Murray? I'm getting there.

As any respectable nerd knows, there are codes that will let you cheat the video game. Up, up, down, down, left, right, left, right, B, A, Start will get you unlimited free lives in Contra. If we are living in a simulation, can we fuck with it? Are there cheat codes?

I'm reminded of the Super Mario Bros. games. In Super Mario Bros. 2, you could walk through a door to enter Sub-Space and then when you came back, the level had reset itself. The Shy Guy you had just killed would be back, as if nothing had happened. If you repeat a certain action within some games, the program gets confused and replays the original scene.

My buddy Charles Moore has this creepy story he tells at dinner parties. He was a professional runner for some time and used to jog from one side of Cleveland to the other. One morning, he took a different route and encountered a young boy dressed in outdated clothes. The kid was dressed as if he were a newsie from 1920 or something. Well, the kid stopped, looked at him, and then disappeared. Some hear that story and think, *Ghost*. But if the universe is a simulation, maybe what Charles saw was a *glitch*. Maybe he'd reenacted some specific movement and a scene from long ago had been triggered to replay in front of him.

I wanted to trigger a glitch. I would re-create Maura's journey into New Hampshire in as much detail as I could manage. Ostensibly, I did this so that I could observe the things she saw and report on the particulars she experienced the night she disappeared. But on some level, I was entertaining the notion that I might be able to hack the simulation, if such a thing existed. That maybe by going through the same motions that Maura did, I might trip up the part of the code that knows what happened to her. Would I see Maura's "ghost"? Would I see the shadow of her killer offer her a ride?

I drank because Maura drank. The Jameson snuck up on me like it always does. My old editor introduced me to the stuff. Smooth. Woody. Mix it with Coke to stay awake. Sip it to sleep. I drank enough to get tipsy. How drunk was Maura when she got off 91 at Wells River and drove east? They'd found an open box of wine, a bunch of liquor, and a soda bottle that reeked of booze in her wrecked car. Most likely, Maura was tipsier than I was, but I didn't want to push it. I still needed to observe.

It was twilight when I passed through the town of Woodsville, the last bit of red sun sneaking down the other side of the Presidentials. It's one of those logging towns along the Connecticut River, the kind with a row of wooden storefronts on Main Street. In the 1800s, John Woods owned the mill and much of the town's economy revolved around his loggers' favorite vices: drinkin' and fuckin'. Today, Woodsville feels empty. The saloons and whorehouses have become restaurants and stationery stores. But there's this feeling like something's happening in town, that it's just a year or two away from becoming that secret summer spot for rich New Yorkers.

After passing the new Wal-Mart, I found Route 112 immediately on my right. Here, in the beginning, the road is called Wild Ammonoosuc, then it becomes Lost River Road, and finally it's the Kancamagus Highway, named for a fearless leader of the Pennacook Indians, who tried to broker peace with the white folk (spoiler alert: It didn't work out well). The road is two lanes of blacktop, twisty along the mountain valley where the Ammonoosuc River trails beside the northern shoulder. It was dark, real dark, by the time I got there. I checked the clock: 6:49. That was strange. I had left Amherst as late as the police figured Maura could have departed, but I had arrived here about forty minutes before the time of her accident, which was reported to police dispatch at 7:27.

That was too much missing time for a simple gas station refill. Maura must have taken a break somewhere along the way. Had she gone to a restaurant for dinner? Had she stopped to meet someone?

When I said that Wild Ammonoosuc Road was "twisty," I was underplaying it a bit. The road bends along the natural swoop of the river and it's a bitch to drive at night if you are unfamiliar with its pattern. There are no streetlights. The only illumination comes from isolated homes along the way: squat cabins, dilapidated trailers, low ranches obscured by snow.

I was looking for a "weathered barn." In the newspaper

accounts of Maura's accident, the turn where she slid off the road is marked by a weathered barn. There's a giant blue ribbon tied to a tree near the crash site. I drove slow.

I thought about another of the world's greatest mysteries—an abduction, no less—that occurred not far from here on a similar cold, dark night in 1961. Returning from vacation in Montreal, Betty and Barney Hill spotted a strange aircraft over the mountains while en route to Portsmouth. Curious, they followed the light into Franconia Notch, just below the Old Man in the Mountain. It was there, Betty and Barney later claimed, that they were abducted by the crew of a spaceship—humanoid aliens from the Zeta Reticuli star system. It's the sort of story you laugh at during the day. But, at night, you can't help but wonder. . . .

A turn appeared quickly out of the dark. My tires lost traction. *Turn into the skid,* I heard my old man say. I course-corrected and came out of the drift. Surely that turn was where Maura had left the road. But there was no weathered barn that I could see. Maybe it was back a ways, beyond the reach of my headlights. But there was no blue ribbon, either. Not here.

I drove back to the beginning of the Wild Ammonoosuc and tried again. Somehow, I ended up on French Pond Road this time, heading into the town of Swiftwater. *Goddamn it.* The dash read 7:45 and I still had no idea where this weathered barn was. I searched for another half hour, then gave up.

I made my way back to the Wells River Motel, across the border into Vermont. This hotel was the headquarters for the search for Maura Murray in 2004, a humble one-story white ranch building with theme rooms. The owner put me in the Teddy Bear Suite—beggars can't be choosers. I got properly drunk and spent the night surrounded by stuffed bears, angry with myself for thinking I could trick the universe. What had I expected would happen? That the man Maura's family believed abducted her would drive by and offer me a ride the same way he'd done for her, seven years ago?

ELEVEN

Never Take Rides from Strangers

I awoke the next morning to one of those fuzzy headaches where everything looks like it's coming at you through a bronze filter. Took a warm shower. Shaved. Called home. Then I checked out of the motel and drove into Woodsville for breakfast at Shiloh's, one of those catchall country diners that can still be found in the vast, empty spaces between cities. After some coffee and eggs I got back in the car and gave it another try.

I got my first real view of the White Mountains that morning. I was born and raised in Northeast Ohio, where the land is flat except for where it buckles up around the Cuyahoga River. My hometown was a pretty place to explore on the back of a Huffy bike, but I would never use the word "grandeur" when describing it. This part of New Hampshire, though . . . it fit into that part of my mind reserved for visions of Mirkwood and the foothills of the Lonely Mountain from *The Hobbit*. Back in Akron, I could take nature for granted. Here, nature persists. It clamors for your attention: the wide, frozen rivers; the expansive farms; the hills of pine that roll like waves all the way to the horizon. I was struck by the new colors of the trees and rocks and grass and water, as if I had been living in a three-color world and suddenly I had been transported into one of those new TVs, the ones with the fourth color that makes everything more vibrant. I was affected, too, by the size of the world, the distance I could see. That is grandeur: *size*. Mount Washington loomed over everything, the highest peak east of the Mississippi, 6,288 feet above sea level. It was formed primarily by the Laurentide Ice Sheet, which carved great gulches through New Hampshire twenty-five thousand years ago, and it's capped in rock and snow and ice. The mountain serves as the boundary between the northern Presidential range and its gentler, southerly sisters. The Native Americans called this mountain Agiocochook or Waumbeket Methna. This is history, and even sociopaths like me feel humility before it.

The drive along Wild Ammonoosuc Road was a different journey in the morning light, sober. This time, I kept going long after it felt as though I must have passed the place where Maura had crashed. On my left, the Swiftwater Stage Shop went by, a combo fill-up station and small grocery inside an old cabin. About a mile later, I found the weathered barn.

It's not really weathered, this barn. It's painted red and white and there's a gravel lot beside it. It sits off the road at a sharp turn, almost a 90-degree bend. In the winter, the snowbanks are packed into glacial walls by the plows. Just after the barn, I spotted a giant blue ribbon tied to a thin fir tree. The story goes that Fred Murray had put the first ribbon there but that it had been replaced by family members and friends over the years, a quiet memorial to the missing woman, a reminder to locals that someone still cared.

I tried to imagine how the accident might have happened,

how Maura had ended up in the snowbank on the right side, facing back the way she'd come. Early reports said she'd likely slid at
the turn and crashed into the shoulder. But I couldn't make that
work in my mind. The centrifugal forces that gripped the car after
the curve should not have allowed for this. Maybe she'd bounced
from one side to the other, like a bearing in a pinball machine.
(Granted, I'm no physicist.)

I turned around at Bradley Hill Road, a T-intersection about
three hundred feet beyond the blue-ribbon tree, and then parked
in the gravel lot behind the weathered barn. I retrieved my camera
from the backseat and walked to the crash site. As I snapped away,
a red car pulled up beside me and stopped. I waved at the driver, an
old man hunched over the wheel. He rolled down his window.

"You here for Maura Murray?" he asked.

"Yes," I said.

"Well, I know what happened to her."

"You do?"

He nodded. "Hop in and I'll show you."

Now, in hindsight, I realize how this looks. It's a hundred
kinds of bad, is it not? We're taught in preschool that we should
never, ever accept rides from strangers. And I suppose that goes
double for strangers who show up at a crime scene. Obviously, I'm
not getting into this man's car.

"Can you just tell me?" I asked.

"No. I have to show you."

"Can I follow you in my car?"

The old man shook his head. "That'll take too long. You interested or what? I have things to do."

"Let me lock up," I said.

I walked back to my car, reminding myself of all the reasons I
shouldn't be doing what I was about to do. This is the part in the

horror movie where the audience groans because, really, how stupid can a person be?

But . . .

But he was old. Like, really old. Ancient. Looked to be about
ninety. No joke. I'm not a big guy but I thought I could take a
ninety-year-old man. Also, what are the chances, right? Would
a serial killer really come back to the scene of the crime and ask a
reporter to get into his car so that he could kill him, too? That's
ridiculous.

I wrote the man's license plate number in my notebook and
then slipped it under the driver's seat. He probably wouldn't murder me and use my skin for a man-suit, but if he did, I wanted
someone to find him.

I got into the old man's car and buckled my seat belt. He
turned around and drove east.

"What's your name?" I asked.

"Ain't gonna tell you my name," he said.

Christ, I thought. *Enough with the melodrama.* "So what happened to Maura Murray?"

"I'll show you what I think happened," he said, keeping his
eyes on the road. His car had that smell cars get when you don't
clean them too often: dirt and grime, not really unpleasant. "That
year, the snow was built up just like it is now. Enough snow on the
ground you could track a person if they walked in it."

He nodded to the left, at a ranch home with wood siding and
a rack of antlers above the garage door. "That's Butch's place. Or
was," he said. Butch Atwood: the bus driver, the last person to
speak to Maura before she disappeared. "Butch had an antique
business, you know? Flea market. Sold old glass bottles, that sort of
thing. He was sitting in his bus there, out front of the garage with
a clear view of the girl's car. He would have seen if she'd taken a

ride with somebody. And maybe she did. And maybe the person he saw her get a ride with was someone he was ascared of. The person I have in mind is capable of threatening Butch."

"Who was it?"

The old man didn't answer. We had been driving east for several minutes now, and had not passed another road. Just dense forest on the right, river on the left. If Maura had come running this way after the accident, there would have been no place for her to hide when another driver came along.

"Where in the world could someone hide a dead body around here?" I said.

"I'll show you," he said with a smile.

Finally, we came to another road that hooked right, up the mountain.

"This is Route 116," he said. "Rough country round here. Ah, here you go." The old man pulled his car to the side, by a guardrail. We got out and walked over to the ledge. We were on a short bridge above a deep gulley. Twenty feet below, a torrent of clear water shot around giant boulders crusted with ice, snaking down the mountain toward the Ammonoosuc.

"Right here's a good place," he said, looking into the gulley. "You could throw a body into that brook and it would keep in the ice until the thaw and then it would wash away down the river when the ice broke up."

We stared at the water for some time and then returned to his car. We continued farther up Route 116.

"There was a woman's body found in a brook in Swiftwater some years ago," he said. "Epileptic woman, did work for this fella I want to tell you about. Housekeeping. I heard there was a pickup spotted by the girl's accident that night. This fella, he drives a black pickup. He gets to drinking sometimes. And when he drinks, he gets mean."

We stopped at a private drive that led farther up the mountain. But the old man didn't say anything.

"Is this where he lives?" I asked.

The old man drove on. "I told you all I can tell you," he said. "It may be all well. Maybe nothing to it. I just had something flash over my mind. That's all."

A few minutes later we arrived back at the weathered barn and he left me by my car. He didn't say anything else. Just shook my hand and went on his way. I've thought about this encounter a lot over the years. And I'm still at a loss. Oh, I tracked him down, eventually. Used his license plate. I discovered he had a property dispute with the man he accused. That's probably all it is—just bad blood between two weird men. But . . . I wonder.

When he was out of sight, I continued east down the Kancamagus Highway, making for Route 93. I could take it south into Eastern Mass. From there, it was a straight shot to Hanson, where Maura Murray was a legend long before her disappearance.

TWELVE

The Runner

I like Hanson. It reminds me of home. The roads are wide and the houses are not too close together. Lots of ponds for fishing and a couple places to get freezer meat and beer. Teens still party in the woods and ride dirt bikes over at "the pits" and hang out at the BK. People here live for Friday night football. Not so close to the ocean that you have to think about it all the time. I found this restaurant on Route 58, the Olde Hitching Post, that serves everything from Yankee Pot Roast to Shrimp Pignoli. I ordered crab cakes and a Diet Coke, and then drove out to Maura's high school, Whitman-Hanson Regional.

This wasn't the school Maura knew. This brand-new sprawling brick campus sits where the old cross-country course once was. But Maura is still a presence here. A records board hangs on the wall by the gym. The Murray girls are all over it. Julie and Maura hold the records for the 3.1-mile. In 1997, Julie ran a 19:10. Maura did it in 18:58. Julie was first. But Maura was better.

In the athletic office, I found two coaches who remembered Maura. Coach Mike Driscoll's face lit up when he talked about his star runner. "She was extremely driven," he said. "She always wanted to be the best. Her freshman year, she broke the record in the two-mile. I thought, *Wow! She's got big things going for her.* Then she kind of matured and her speed was never the same. What she had was endurance. She was an icon."

Coach Keith Erwin, a young man with clipped dark hair, went to school with Maura. He was a senior when she was a freshman. "She was very soft-spoken," he recalled. "But she would give you the shirt off her back."

"The last time I saw her," said Driscoll, "she was running for UMass. She seemed so happy to be away from West Point."

Both men remember Maura's father. Fred was the constant shadow behind both girls.

"Fred was a pretty good baseball coach around here when I was growing up," said Driscoll. "His teams were always the best. Fred coached Maura, too. He was always leading her in extra workouts. She adored her father. She would do anything for him."

"You would always see her dad at races," said Erwin. "And sometimes, I'd see Maura out at Luddam's Ford, fishing from the shore with Fred."

When news of Maura's disappearance made its way to Hanson, her coaches were shocked, but hopeful.

"Honestly," said Driscoll, "I hope she was meeting someone up there and that she's still around."

I thought that was an odd statement to make, given the things they'd just told me about Maura's relationship with Fred. If she had run away, why wouldn't she tell her father?

THIRTEEN

Private Eyes

Few people know the particulars of Maura's story as well as John Healy. When I interviewed him, he was sixty-two and retired from the state police, a grizzled man with a high forehead, a gumshoe from central casting. When her case first threatened to go cold, Healy mustered a group of private eyes to reevaluate the mystery. I gave him a call shortly after returning to Ohio, and he gave me an earful. He was living in a house in the woods of Warner, New Hampshire. At the time, he was busy trying to get a convicted rapist out of prison.

"He didn't do it," said Healy. "This broad made it up. I put a lot of people in jail when I was a cop. I can't sit by and let an innocent man rot in prison. That sticks in my craw. This one, it sticks with you, too. Maura's disappearance. And, for me, it was about my daughter, Melissa. She's blind in one eye. One day she was sitting in her room at college and she looks up and a black guy is standing there. He got scared. Backed out, disappeared. There but for the grace of God goes my daughter. I needed to do this case. I don't know if I did it for the Murray family or me."

The first thing Healy did was talk to Jeffery Strelzin, the chief prosecutor for the New Hampshire AG's office. He'd known Strelzin when the lawyer was a teenager. Healy wanted his blessing before starting. After he got it, Healy e-mailed other private eyes in his organization, expecting to hear back from a couple. A dozen responded, a civilian force to rival the official investigation.

"I went out to the scene to get a feel for the area. Then we conducted interviews. Did backgrounds on everybody. We interviewed the entire fire department who responded to the accident the night Maura disappeared."

Then came the ground searches. Healy explained how the volunteer searches you see on TV news reports are logistical nightmares. To do it well, you need to feed and house the volunteers. Medical staff should be on hand for emergencies. Then there's the problem of communication. Everyone needs a charged walkie-talkie. You need a staff just to organize the volunteers, to corral them into grid patterns, and to take a head count at the end of the day. The searches for Maura Murray's body—because that's what they were looking for by then—were daunting due to the mountainous terrain: deep gullies; wide rivers; steep drop-offs. Unforgiving country. A family donated their summer home to house his crew. A school provided beds for twenty men. Merchants delivered free water. They set up a command post with a private area for the Murrays, out at the Mountain Lakes estates.

Healy also brought in cadaver dogs. "The dogs hit on a piece of rug in an abandoned A-frame house," said Healy. "It was an empty house and the former resident had a history of domestic violence. It was probably drops from bloody noses. I'm ninety percent sure it had nothing to do with the case, but I still sent the information to police."

Healy and his team developed a more accurate time line of the moments surrounding Maura's disappearance. Based on the 911 calls and the logbooks of the cops who arrived on scene, Maura vanished quickly. "The window of opportunity between the human who last saw her, Butch Atwood, and when the police arrived and found her missing was three to five minutes."

One night, Healy parked at the weathered barn and counted cars to see how often someone drove by. Between seven and eight o'clock he counted a total of eight cars, almost all of which turned onto Bradley Hill Road, across from Butch Atwood's house. "The chances of someone just driving by are very, very remote, unless they lived there," he said. "There's no destination around there. It's very dark, very rural for miles. Not a lot going on. No cell phone service."

Word on the street was that Maura had traveled into the North Country to commit suicide atop Mount Washington. "The rumor started because Maura gave her nursing scrubs away before she left Amherst, and giving away possessions is something suicides do just before. But what happened was she had borrowed those scrubs. She was just returning them."

When Healy spoke to Kathleen about that odd phone call the night of her sister's breakdown, he had trouble getting any solid information out of her. "You can't really talk to Kathleen," he explained. "She was drunk that night and she was drunk when I tried to talk to her about it."

It took a year of working the case before Healy became convinced that Maura had not run away. He believed stress in Maura's life had percolated until the young woman simply needed a mental health day, a chance to get away, set her mind right. "I think Maura was scared that she was becoming her sister."

Healy believes Maura was murdered. And he thinks some witnesses saw more than they let on.

"Like that shithead Butch Atwood," Healy growled. "He gave three different versions of what happened that night. In one story, he got out of the bus to talk to Maura. In another, she was still in the car with the air bag in her face. In another, she was standing outside the car when they spoke."

Before Atwood died, Healy traveled to Florida to interrogate him.

"He came to the door. Would not shake my hand. He just stood there, arms crossed. He didn't answer any of my questions."

Atwood told Healy that he'd once been a cop, too. But Healy knew that the closest Butch had ever come to being a man in blue was working for the Department of Fish and Game.

"He must have seen what happened to Maura," said Healy. "I believe he was concealing the person who did it. And that person was someone Butch was afraid of." But Healy wouldn't tell me who.

That statement gave me a shiver. It was the same thing the old man in the red car had told me.

Another person Healy tried to contact was Rick Forcier, a contractor who lived in the trailer across the street from Butch. Several months after Maura went missing, Forcier came forward with a story about seeing a woman running east, down Wild Ammonoosuc Road, the night of the crash. He told police he'd only just now figured that it might be important info.

"Forcier was a strange puppy," said Healy. "We asked to search his property, but he wouldn't let us."

Then Healy dropped a detail that might change the entire dynamic of Maura's last drive. He didn't think the damage to Maura's car matched the accepted story of the crash. The Saturn's hood was bent inward from above, on the driver's side, and yet the headlight was not broken. "I do not believe that was the first accident Maura had that night," said Healy. "The damage is consistent with a car running into the back of a semi, as if she hit it high on her bumper, when it was stationary. It's another piece of the mystery."

We talked for more than an hour, going over the minutiae of the case, and Healy hardly paused to catch his breath. He loved talking about this riddle. It was only when I asked about Fred Murray that Healy got quiet for a moment.

"Fred's in a world of his own," he said. "He's a volatile man. I remember he was at the Wells River Motel one day and I came in the room to speak to another investigator. I tried to talk to Fred, but he acted like I wasn't even there. I can't fault the man. I don't know how I'd act."

Days into the search for his daughter, Fred became hostile toward the local police, telling the media that the detectives were dragging their feet when they should be actively looking for the dirtbag who took his daughter. Healy thinks his open relationship with the detectives was something Fred took as an insult. Why share info with the police if the police weren't sharing anything with the family?

Being close with both sides, Healy knew when Fred lied to the press. Maura left West Point because she wanted to become a nurse, Fred would say when interviewed.

"But I was told that when Maura left West Point it was not under the best circumstances," said Healy. "It wasn't just for a career change."

FOURTEEN

What Really Happened at West Point

"When something tragic happens, you don't really want to say anything bad about the person. But everyone has skeletons in their closet." That's how Megan Sawyer began the conversation.

Megan was a friend of Maura's at West Point, a fellow runner, another young woman trying to power through the military academy's tough regimen. She reached out to me when she heard I was working on Maura's case and offered to provide a few answers.

Megan was standing beside Maura when Maura got busted for stealing makeup from the commissary at Fort Knox. Yes: She attempted to shoplift from the most secure military facility in the United States. The MPs got her. Back at the dorms, Maura confided to Megan about the theft. "It was so stupid," she said. "I only took five dollars' worth of stuff."

Usually, Maura was quiet, Megan said. This was the most personal she'd ever gotten. "But you could tell there were some inner demons. She seemed sad." She was also "insanely smart." So smart, said Megan, that Maura often helped older sister Julie with homework.

The daily routine back at the academy was harsh. Everyone had chores and duties. Most days, you woke up around 4:30 A.M. Clean bathrooms, take out the trash. Every day cadets had to read the newspaper front-to-back and you might be quizzed on current events. Outside of class (and conditioning for the track team), there was not much extra time.

The dorms were coed. Two or three women would share a room, next to a roomful of men. In such close quarters, Maura's bulimia was no secret. Megan heard her purging on more than one occasion. "She had issues with loving herself."

This lent credence to a story a private investigator told me about what happened at Thanksgiving the year before Maura disappeared. Her mother, Laurie, had made fun of her in front of family members. She'd said, "Why did you make so much food if you're just going to throw it up later?"

Maura got a lot of stress from her sister Julie too. Megan told me that Julie could be tough on her kid sister, that she would belittle Maura for not studying enough, not running harder.

Megan said that Helena Dwyer-Murray, the family spokesperson, told her to keep quiet about Maura's troubles. "She told me, 'Don't say these negative things. Watch what you tell people.' " The message was clear: It doesn't matter what happened to her in the past; the only thing that matters is that Maura is missing now.

During her time at West Point, Maura went through basic military training, including survival skills. She could operate the machine gun on top of a tank. Based on what she knew of Maura, Megan believed her friend had what it took to start a new life.

"If she wanted to make up another identity, she could do it," says Megan. "If she wanted to disappear, she could. She never wanted to look bad in front of people. I think she probably thought, *If I just disappeared, they wouldn't think badly of me.* I believe she's alive. It's just a feeling I've always had."

FIFTEEN

Cracks in the Façade

"I want to look for Maura's body after I interview the detective, so I might not be back for a while," I said. This was the summer of 2011, and my wife, Julie, and I were staying at the Nootka Lodge, a retro log-cabin motel in Woodsville, while I did research on the book. The lead investigator in the first weeks of Maura's disappearance had finally agreed to meet me.

"Well, have fun," she said, sarcastically, on my way out.

What would I do if I really did find her body, though? I wondered as I drove around Mount Washington that day. I'd seen dead bodies. Plenty. But only in autopsy photographs or in cushioned coffins at the end of a receiving line. Never outside. Never decaying. Never up close. I didn't particularly want to go into the woods, searching. But I'd come all that way. I had to look. If only to make sure nothing was there. But first—Scarinza.

In the beginning, John Scarinza was the face of the investigation, a spokesman for the state police; you'll see him in those television specials on YouTube. I drove halfway across New Hampshire to meet with Scarinza. We got together at an out-of-the-way community building near his home. We sat at a conference table and talked about the case. Retirement suits Scarinza. He has the look of a young grandfather who still enjoys fishing and hiking, manly stuff, drives a big-ass truck.

For Scarinza, the mystery began at 6 A.M. Wednesday, two days after Maura's abandoned car was discovered in Haverhill. That's when he got the call from the local police chief, asking for help. An assumed drunk-driving incident was starting to look like something more.

"Put yourself in his shoes," said Scarinza, defending Haverhill police chief Jeff Williams. "It's not an unusual occurrence, finding abandoned cars after having too much to drink up here. That's what it looked like. The officer on scene observes a box of wine that has spilled inside. The driver is gone. If you've had too much to drink, you don't want to sit down with law enforcement. But usually, you expect them to call in to the police the next morning, after they sobered up, looking for their car."

When the police couldn't reach Fred Tuesday morning, they got a warrant to open and search Maura's vehicle. Inside, they found a book titled *Not Without Peril*. "It's an . . . interesting book," he said.

Not Without Peril was written by a journalist named Nicholas Howe, who, before he took to writing, worked for the Appalachian Mountain Club, protecting hikers on the Presidential Range. Howe rescued people who tried to tackle Mount Washington in the winter. *Not Without Peril* traces the most famous deaths ever to occur on the mountain, beginning with Frederick Strickland (the son of an English aristocrat) in 1849. It's a bit prosaic unless you are an avid hiker, but I think what Scarinza meant when he said "interesting" is that the book is mainly about the fame that comes with dying on Mount Washington. When you die near the summit, your name is recorded in a ledger, revered by generations of hikers who make the pilgrimage each year. Your death *means* something if it happens there. There's a sense of immortality that goes with it.

"Sometime mid-afternoon on Tuesday, Fred calls in to Haverhill police and explains that it's his daughter's car they have," the detective continued. "His first sense is that Maura has gone to the North Country to commit suicide—to go off and die 'like an old squaw' is what he said to the police."

Chief Williams called Scarinza on Wednesday morning to see if the state police could get a chopper in the air. Scarinza reached out to New Hampshire Fish and Game, which had a helicopter equipped with FLIR cameras—military-grade, "forward-looking infrared" scopes, Scarinza explained. Soon, he was flying over Wild Ammonoosuc Road. I got a sense he enjoyed that part.

"What you could see is what you couldn't see," he said. "I remember seeing this gorgeous red fox that stuck out against the snow below. You could see deer stands in the area. I'm seeing deer tracks in the snow. Just great detail. I would have seen human footprints in a second. It was good, clean snow and it hadn't snowed since the accident. It made for good search conditions." But there were no human tracks. Maura did not walk into the woods.

Regardless, Scarinza said that the hills and valleys around Mount Washington were a good place to get lost. He recalled a case from early in his career where a woman from Massachusetts drove into the mountains and left a note behind saying she was going to kill herself. Fish and Game did an extensive search but couldn't find her. Seven years later, a hiker stepped off the path to take a leak and found her skeleton. She'd sat down on a log, taken a bunch of pills, and then fallen backward onto the ground.

In the summer of 2004, the state police conducted a second, more extensive search of the area—eighty troopers on the ground and a Fish and Game helicopter in the air. When the team discovered a skeleton at the top of Mount Kancamagus, Scarinza thought the mystery was solved. "I mean, it would be a huge coincidence to find someone else's skeleton during the search for Maura Murray," he said. "But it ended up being a man who disappeared twenty years ago."

These mountains are a kind of Mecca for people thinking about ending it. It's the closest you can get to Heaven east of the Mississippi, after all.

The state police took a bloodhound to the scene of the accident and used a "scent article" from Maura's car to get the dog to follow her trail.

"The bloodhound went a hundred yards east and then appeared to lose track of her scent," said Scarinza. "Does that mean she got into a vehicle there? Perhaps. Does it mean that enough time had gone by that it wasn't a scent opportunity for the dog? Perhaps."

In the summer, Maura and Fred often visited Jigger Johnson, a campsite just a little ways farther down the Kancamagus Highway, he said. They'd go hiking and share a tent. Sometimes, Fred splurged for a cabin in Bartlett. Sometimes Maura's younger brother would join them, but mostly it was just Maura and Fred.

When detectives asked specific questions about Maura's past, though, Fred stopped cooperating with the investigation. "We asked, 'What's going on in her life that would cause her to leave UMass?' Fred said, 'It's not important. She's missing. Find her.'

But if we understood why she left, maybe we could understand where she was going."

Fred would know better than anyone else Maura's state of mind in the days leading up to her disappearance. He'd visited his daughter that weekend. He was with her the morning before she drove into New Hampshire.

"Fred comes down to Amherst," said Scarinza, replaying the days leading up to Maura's journey. "They're all drinking quite a bit. Father goes to his hotel. Maura has his car. She leaves a party to go back to Fred's hotel at three in the morning. Gets into a single-car accident. Why she doesn't get arrested for drunk driving is beyond me. And why is she going to his hotel at that time a night? She has a dorm room. It's weird."

Clearly something was troubling Maura. By all appearances, when she left on Monday, Maura was leaving for good. She'd packed her belongings into boxes. On top of the boxes was an e-mail from her boyfriend, Billy. When Scarinza read it, he immediately thought it was a pointed message that Maura had intentionally left behind. "Maura had found out Billy was cheating on her. That's what the e-mail was about."

The more Scarinza looked into Maura's background, the more the image of that "All-American Girl" began to disintegrate. There were reports that Maura had been found passed out, drunk, in the hallways at West Point. She may have had another secret, too.

"The searches she conducted on her computer before she left Amherst suggest Maura may have been pregnant," said Scarinza. Maura visited a number of sites that talked about the dangers of drinking while pregnant. She may not have told anyone yet. "She was a very private person, even with her close friends." He wonders about the phone call that upset her so much the night she was working at Melville Hall. He wonders if her sister Kathleen got the sense that Maura was knocked up; maybe that's what came out in the conversation.

By the time I got involved, the state police had invested six thousand hours in the case. The Department of Fish and Game, the AG's office, the FBI, and the UMass police also devoted time. Scarinza and his team interviewed people in Vermont, Massachusetts, and Maine. Detectives traveled to places like Rochester, New York, to investigate sightings of Maura. The search for Maura Murray was a large operation, and it led nowhere.

"At the point I retired, we didn't even have evidence that Maura was the victim of a crime," said Scarinza. "We're not saying she wasn't. We don't know. Everything that was done was done in the event she was the victim of a crime so that we can present items as evidence later. My sense is that she is not still alive."

I went back to that gulley the man in the red car had driven me to months before, the place he believed some killer had dumped Maura's body. I parked the car and scooted over the guardrail. I found a footpath leading down to the water. It was steep and slow-going, and the thick canopy of oaks and evergreens overhead made it muggy. At the bottom, an icy mountain stream ran between great boulders left behind by the last glacier. The only way to continue was to stand on one boulder and then hop over to the next. The rocks were mossy and slick with runoff and dew. My shirt was soon soaked with sweat and the moisture of the air.

And then the bugs found me. Primordial flies, bigger than any fly should be, landing on my neck and arms. I swatted at them, waved them away, but word got around: There was fresh meat in the gulley.

If someone had deposited Maura's body here, her skeleton

would have been taken farther down the mountain with each spring thaw, when the ice breaks apart and a wave of water washes down to the Ammonoosuc in a violent torrent. There was a lot of junk down here, caught in eddies around fallen trees. I found a miner's pickax. But no skeleton. No shirt or pants. No sign of Maura.

By the time I got back to the car, an hour and a half later, I was in tears from the exertion of the hike. Such a stupid thing to do, alone. If I had slipped on a boulder, broken an ankle, nobody would have heard my screams.

We forget how dangerous nature can be. We want to forget, I think. We don't want to be reminded that nature is more deadly than man. Man can be cruel, but nature is indifferent. It is the unrivaled psychopath.

I needed to be smarter about this investigation. I was already taking stupid risks, and I hadn't even really begun.

SIXTEEN

The Clique

I wanted Julie with me when I went knocking on doors in Hanson. It was time to speak to Maura's friends, and I knew I would get further with my wife beside me than I would alone. Think about it: Here is a story of a missing woman. Murdered, maybe. And a reporter nobody knows has decided to write a book about it. Julie's presence would make me less threatening, the interview not so much an interrogation, more of a friendly visit. It's a tactic I'd used while reporting on the Amy Mihaljevic case with some success.

The coaches I had spoken to told me that Maura's best friend in high school was Liz Drewniak, the valedictorian of their class. Liz was the mother hen to a clique of several girls that included Maura Murray. Attempts to reach her via Facebook had not panned out. So after we left the Nootka Lodge, I drove down to Hanson and dropped in at the Drewniak home. We caught Liz's parents as they were packing their car for a trip to the Cape. They invited us in and served us iced tea.

Liz's mother is an Elizabeth too, goes by Beth. "There were seven of them that hung out together," Beth explained. "Liz and Maura and Andrea Connolly, Carly Muise, Katie Jones, Erin Devine, and Laura Gainey." Katie and Liz were still in the area and Andrea was somewhere in Massachusetts, but the others were out of state or overseas. Fred didn't want the girls to talk to me, said Beth.

"Maura came from a dysfunctional family," Beth explained. The Murrays' marriage fell apart around the time the youngest child, Kurt, was born. "We used to have big birthday parties here. Liz and Maura's birthdays are only a few days apart. One year we heard that Maura was not going to have a birthday party so we thought, Why not have a party for her, too?"

Fred moved away to Weymouth after he separated from Maura's mother, but he often returned to Hanson to work out with his girls. "Fred was always there for them," she said. "I remember seeing Maura and her sister Julie running laps at the school for him on Christmas. He's an intense sort of guy."

Beth remembers Maura as a smart, energetic girl, always with a twinkle in her eyes. "She was hardworking. An incredible athlete. A beautiful girl, but very plain. She didn't wear makeup. She kept things to herself. If there were problems she wouldn't share them, even with her closest friends."

The week she disappeared, one of her friends tried to instant-message Maura to find out where she was. "They asked, 'Where the heck have you been?' And then a message came back: 'This is the police. We're looking for Maura. Do you know where she is?'"

After that, Maura's friends met in Worcester, to put their heads together, see if they could come up with an idea of what

Maura might be up to. They talked about the time Maura went to Boston for the day and never told anyone. They wondered if she could be in Providence, where they liked to go clubbing. One of the girl's aunts had a place in New Hampshire. That's where Maura had partied on New Year's Eve. Was that where she was heading? They all decided to take time off from school and help with the search.

"Liz knew that Maura was in serious trouble when the week was up and she hadn't come back," said Beth. Liz had a breakdown during an interview with Investigation Discovery while filming a segment about the case. Liz hasn't spoken publicly since. "They had to stop the cameras. Afterward, she asked me, 'Where did that come from?' I told her, 'You buried it. It had to come out sometime.'"

That night, my wife and I had dinner at Boston's Union Oyster House, the oldest restaurant in the United States. John F. Kennedy and Daniel Webster dined there. I destroyed some crabs while we talked.

"Sometimes you come off a little obsessive," Julie said, critiquing my interview with the Drewniaks. "You should slow down. Let them talk. And you need to remember to smile. You're too serious. I think it made them nervous."

She was right. I was taking the case too personally, and it was affecting my interviews. This was due, in part, to Fred's refusal to speak to me and his interference with my reporting, telling others not to return my calls. It made things difficult, when all I wanted to do was find his daughter. I needed to remember that these people who knew Maura did not owe me anything. Their friend was missing. Everyone close to Maura was in suspended animation until a body was found. Or until Maura came home.

When leads dry up, sometimes it's helpful to step back and look at the bigger picture. In cases of abduction, police detectives often look to similar crimes that have occurred in the past, in an attempt to find patterns of behavior, to determine if a serial predator might be responsible. Were there any disappearances similar to Maura's in the area?

As a matter of fact, there were.

SEVENTEEN

Molly, Holly, and Bri

A month after Maura disappeared, and ninety miles away, another attractive brunette vanished following what appeared to be an auto accident near a dilapidated farmhouse. Brianna Maitland was seventeen, a wayward soul from East Franklin who talked often of putting that boring, blue-collar region of northern Vermont in her rearview. She had a skinny face and old-soul eyes that could draw in a man from across the room. She worked two jobs: washing dishes at the Black Lantern Inn in Montgomery, and waitressing in St. Albans. On March 19, 2004, Brianna—Bri, to her friends—took the exam for her GED. She left work that night around midnight, skipping dinner with coworkers to get some sleep.

But she never showed up for her shift the next morning. When her roommate returned home two days later, there was no sign that Bri had ever come back from the Black Lantern Inn. Two more days passed before her roommate got worried enough to contact the girl's parents. They hadn't heard from her, either.

Brianna's father, Bruce, and her mother, Kellie, immediately drove to the police station in St. Albans to report her missing. They learned that a state trooper had found Bri's 1985 green Olds two days earlier, crashed into a farmhouse on Route 118. The trooper assumed the car had been abandoned by a drunk driver, and had it towed to an auto shop. Bri's father found her ATM card, migraine meds, and makeup still inside. Fearing the worst, he pried open the trunk with a crowbar, but it was empty.

Bri's disappearance quickly became national news. The phone at her parents' home rang continuously. Most were calls from would-be psychics who salivate over stories like these and offer little in the way of helpful leads—*Your daughter is being held in a barn by a big oak tree; Your daughter was taken to Montreal by a man with a tattoo on his arm;* etc. But one call that Bri's aunt Tammy answered was from a member of Maura Murray's family.

"They were asking if we had found anything," she told reporters with Investigation Discovery.

But detectives could find no link between the two cases. The investigation into Bri's disappearance focused on Bri's friends, who were involved in hard drugs. Bri had recently smoked crack cocaine, too, one told police. One of her alleged suppliers was a New York man named Ramon Ryans, who became the prime suspect after an anonymous tip to the police. They raided Ryans's home and arrested him for the drugs and guns they found inside. Ryans claimed not to really know Bri, even though several of her friends had seen them together. The case has since gone cold.

There's another missing girl some investigators have tried to link to Maura's case. Back in Massachusetts, a half hour from UMass down Route 9, you'll find the town of Warren, which has the best swimming hole for miles around: Comins Pond, a largish body of water regulated by a reservoir. Sixteen-year-old Molly Bish worked as a lifeguard there in the summer of 2000. On the morning of June 27, her mother, Magi, dropped off Molly for another day at the pond. When the first swimmers arrived eight minutes later, they found Molly's water bottle, sandals, and an open first aid kit. But the teenager was gone.

In the fall of 2002, a hunter discovered a blue bathing suit in the woods around Whiskey Hill in Palmer, Mass, a short drive from Warren. An ex-policeman-turned-true-crime-author heard about it and wondered if the suit might have belonged to Molly. He returned to the woods and found the suit. It was Molly's. The remains of her body were discovered scattered nearby.

"She came home, bone by bone," her mother told reporters.

That true crime author, a fellow named Tim McGuigan, believes Molly's abduction and murder may be connected to an even older cold case, the 1993 unsolved abduction of ten-year-old Holly Piirainen. During a visit to her grandparents' cottage in Sturbridge, Holly and her brother visited neighbors to play with their new puppies. Only the brother returned. Holly's shoe was found on the side of the road. Two months later, hunters found the girl's body in the woods.

Here's the kicker: Molly Bish wrote to the Piirainen family, in 1993, when she was just ten years old. "I am very sorry," she wrote. "I wish I could make it up to you. Holly is a very pretty girl. She is almost as tall as me. I wish I knew Holly. I hope they found her."

In the aftermath of their daughter's murder, Molly's parents created the Molly Bish Foundation, to teach children how to stay safe in a dangerous world. Molly's father, John, regularly speaks at cold case training seminars.

After Maura Murray's disappearance went cold, the Molly Bish Foundation partnered with a group of private investigators, led by a Massachusetts P.I. named Tom Shamshak, to offer help finding new clues in Maura's case. They worked closely with Fred Murray to find his daughter.

It was around this time that Fred declared war on the State of New Hampshire.

EIGHTEEN

Murray v. State of New Hampshire

Let's talk about Fred Murray a bit.

Think of every Boston cliché. That's Fred Murray. A drinker. Ruddy Irish complexion. A forehead meant for bashing skulls. Shock of thin white hair. People I spoke to described Fred as "volatile" or "a bit of a hothead." Flashes of that temper can be found in the articles published after Maura's disappearance, and the vitriol only intensified as time went on. He has a particular way of speaking and you can almost hear that thick-as-baked-beans Southie accent in the words the reporters found fit to print.

"These guys can't catch a cold," Fred told the UMass student newspaper in 2005. He was talking about the detectives who were searching for his daughter. The cops were dragging their feet, he said, because they didn't want to admit that there was a serial killer in town. "There's a bad guy on their turf. The skunk is on their doorstep."

Fred wanted to know what the detectives had done, whom

they'd spoken to. He sent Freedom of Information requests to the prosecutor's office. Here's a list of some of the items Fred requested:

- A copy of the ATM video from the Amherst bank where Maura withdrew cash.
- The surveillance video from the liquor store.
- An inventory of items provided to police by members of the Murray family.
- A copy of the computer hard drive from Maura's dorm.

But they refused to release any information because it was an open investigation. So Fred wrote to newly elected New Hampshire governor John Lynch:

"I get nearly physically sick when I wake up each morning and the thought of how really little effort it would have taken to rescue my daughter automatically flashes through my mind," he wrote. "It has been over three months since her disappearance and the only leads developed have been handed to the state police by others. Yet still these guys maintain that they don't need any help."

Both Assistant Attorney General David W. Ruoff and Jeffery Strelzin, head of the AG's homicide division, replied to Murray's requests and reminded him that the files were investigatory notes, exempt from public records requests.

In another letter to the governor, Fred asked Lynch to compel the police and prosecutors to release evidence in the case. "With no informational resources available I am left to desperately search for Maura all by myself. How can I do this if the police sit idly on the applicable evidence? Take, for example, her computer. If I could get it back, I might be able to discern who she contacted on that last afternoon and perhaps discover a new direction to follow.

It's one thing if Troop F isn't willing to be part of the solution, but please don't allow them to continue to be part of the problem."

When that didn't work, Fred ambushed the governor. He approached Lynch at the statehouse, with several television cameras in tow. The stunt got him a sit-down with the governor, but law enforcement officials steadfastly refused to release their files because they did not want to jeopardize their investigation. So Fred just sued fucking *everybody*. Named in his civil suit were the governor, the attorney general, the commander of Troop F, and practically every department that had ever worked on Maura's case. The court proceedings began in Grafton County Superior Court in January of 2006.

Representing Fred was Tim Ervin, an attorney from Lowell, Mass, who also reps Bob Marley's estate on issues of copyright and intellectual property.

The superior court wasn't having it. The court upheld the opinion of the detectives and did not release any information to Fred. So Ervin appealed and the case went to the state supreme court. This time, Ervin kicked a little ass. Their case set a public records precedent. *Murray v. State of New Hampshire* now compels law enforcement agencies in New Hampshire to go into greater detail about why certain records cannot be released. It forced the state police to go through their entire case file on Maura Murray's disappearance and explain why each bit of information should be kept secret. This resulted in affidavits from a detective and an assistant attorney general that shed light on the investigation. Fred finally got some documents—a fraction of the file on his daughter, sure, but his lawsuit will help countless journalists and private investigators for decades to come.

I spent $450 to purchase all the documents related to *Murray v. State of New Hampshire*. Reams of paper arrived on my doorstep one day and I spent a week reading through the volumes, parsing out important details and clues.

It quickly became apparent that Fred's argument that the police were not actively investigating his daughter's disappearance was without merit. Detectives had compiled 2,938 records and hoped to use that information in future criminal cases. This included 254 source contacts, 106 interviews with witnesses, and reports from 66 separate law enforcement officials, including detectives from Vermont, New York, and Maine. A grand jury had been convened to issue subpoenas. There were search warrants. Police had gathered credit card history on a number of individuals, run background checks.

The documents also revealed that police had given four polygraph examinations, though the identity of the people interrogated and the results of the tests remained secret.

Most intriguing was the mention of a "one-party intercept." This often means a wiretap.

"The Maura Murray investigation is open and ongoing," Troop F sergeant Todd Landry wrote in his affidavit. "Based on my experience with criminal investigations and the information in this case in particular, I have a reasonable belief that this investigation may lead to criminal charges." Assistant AG Jeffery Strelzin put the likelihood of charging someone with a crime at 75 percent.

During the appeal, Sergeant Landry answered a few specific questions on the stand. On cross, Ervin pushed Landry to reveal the target of his investigation.

"But at this point in time, is there currently a person of interest that the state is looking at with regard to the Maura Murray case?" asked Ervin.

"I think that's a little too close, counsel," the judge said. "If he says there's a specific person, I think that kind of defeats the purpose of the kind of cloak that they're attempting to—"

Prosecutor Nancy Smith, who represented the State of New Hampshire, spoke up. Revealing anything more about Landry's investigation, even in general terms, might identify suspects from a small community, she said. "The people—the identity of those people is fairly well-known."

It seemed Ervin had his answer. "Is the investigation into those individuals currently ongoing?" he asked Landry.

"Yes," he said.

But if police had a prime suspect (or suspects), who was it? And why couldn't they share that info with Fred?

Here's an interesting loophole in public records policy: Typically, as Fred discovered, reports related to an ongoing investigation are kept secret until charges are filed. However, his appeal forced the police to provide documents they could not argue would prove detrimental to their case if Fred were to see them. This included Fred's personal statement to UMass police. After all, Fred knew about this document already; why shouldn't it be provided? And once a record is released, it has to be released to everyone. Including me. I finally had Fred's version of events during that weekend before his daughter vanished.

"We were going to get her a car," Fred said in his signed statement. "That is why I came up that weekend. We started in Hadley looking at cars, four-thousand dollars on my person." Fred explained that he'd withdrawn the four thousand dollars in cash from several different ATMs on the way to UMass. Why didn't he just write a check? I wondered. They never did buy a car that weekend and he has never revealed what happened to the money.

After looking for cars, he said, they picked up Maura's friend Kate Markopoulos and drove to the Amherst Brewing Company and had a few drinks. Then Maura drove him back to the Quality Inn and returned to campus for a party.

"Maura was in bed when I woke up around 10 A.M. Maura woke around ten thirty. She told me about the accident." Remember, Maura had crashed Fred's Toyota on the way back to his hotel at three in the morning. Fred found a rental car to use to get back to Bridgeport and had his Toyota shipped to North Amherst Motors for repairs. Maura felt bad for letting him down, he recalled. "At the motel she said, 'This is the worst.' We went back to the dorm. I told her, 'It'll get fixed.' She went into the dorm, sort of slumped her way in." Maura was supposed to go to the police station on Monday and pick up the accident report for the insurance company and then call Fred with an update. "I was sure she would call, because she wouldn't let me down again. Late the next afternoon [Tuesday], I got a call from my daughter Kathleen telling me Maura hit a tree and was missing."

The UMass officer who filed Fred's report was curious to know if Fred had provided the alcohol Maura took with her to the campus party the night of the accident. First, Fred denied it. Then he said he remembered going to Liquors 44 with Kate and Maura and telling them to pick up some wine but didn't know if that had happened before or after the brewery.

The reports show the growing frustration of detectives as they tried to get information from Fred about what happened to Maura in the days leading up to her disappearance. Fred said further detail wasn't important. He wouldn't say anything more about Maura's past, or his own. Even the reporters covering the case got frustrated.

From an article in the *Whitman-Hanson Express*: "One line Fred repeated throughout the day was, 'It doesn't matter.' If you ask what he did for a living, or why Maura packed her things, or didn't tell anyone where she was headed, he'll just answer, 'It doesn't matter. We'll never know why she came up here.'"

In an interview with Boston's WCVB, Fred said, "It doesn't matter what brought her here to this point. Once she got here, something happened."

Healy and Scarinza told me that Fred refused to sit down for a formal interview with homicide detectives for two and a half years. When he finally agreed to do so, he brought his lawyers with him.

NINETEEN

My Baker Street Irregulars

There's an old truism that goes, "Nobody wants to know how the sausage is made." You hear it a lot in J-school, in circlejerk classes like Media of Mass Communication. What it means is that readers don't want to know the details about how a reporter gathers information; all they care about is the story.

This may have been true when those editors were students. There was a time when the news was relatively unbiased, when you were not watching *liberal* news or *conservative* news, but *news*. Just news. Facts related to you by a friendly voice or simple words on the page. People like Geraldo Rivera and Rush Limbaugh were early adapters of slanted journalism, but the paradigm didn't change until Fox News became a thing. Now you cannot watch the news or read the newspaper, not responsibly anyway, without wondering what the agenda of the writer, or producer, may be.

We may not have cared to know how the sausage was made in a time when we were guaranteed the meat was Grade A. But now some people are putting horseshit in there. Not to beat a dead metaphor.

In the last ten years, the average reader of news became aware of this. I think that's why you see so much suspicion from commenters online. Once, we held journalists in high regard. Hell, Superman was a reporter. But we've come to distrust them. What's their angle?

I've come to believe there's only one way to establish credibility with readers, and that is to show them how you're making the sausage. I think reporters should open up their research to all those interested and bring them along for the ride. That means scanning and posting the supporting documents you use to gather your facts. But I think it should go further. What I'd like to see is an open-sourced form of reporting, where journalists put notes and documents and pictures and sources in something like a readable Google doc as they are reporting.

Maura's case was a good chance to test this idea. After all, she disappeared the same week Facebook launched—hers is the first great mystery of the social media age.

When I began to seriously investigate Maura Murray's disappearance, I decided to open up my research to readers. In June of 2011, I created a blog. A Maura blog. As I interviewed new people, I posted summaries of our conversations online. When I received documents, I scanned them in so that any armchair sleuth could pick them apart.

The blog took off. People contacted me with new leads, new avenues of investigation I hadn't considered. Some readers found details in documents that I had overlooked. Sometimes I used the blog to pose questions like, "Would it be possible to disappear in America today?" And I would get e-mails with links to documented stories of people who faked their own abductions. Better yet, sometimes I got e-mails from the people themselves, anecdotes of how they had considered running away when they were Maura's age and how they would have done it. I wrote back and forth with a man on Reddit who had walked away from his life just to escape from his family.

Whenever Sherlock Holmes needed information, he asked an army of poor street kids to put their ears to the ground. The Baker Street Irregulars, he called them. He knew the kids could cover more ground than any one man. I came to think of these online sleuths as my own Irregulars.

It wasn't just online sleuths, though. The blog was a lightning rod, pulling in sources close to the case whom I had not yet met. A couple weeks after the blog was up and running, I got a call on my cell phone from an unknown number. At the time I noted that the voice had a very distinct timbre. I wrote that he sounded like a rather large, well-educated African-American.

"I've been reading your blog," he said. "I respect what you're doing. And there's information that needs to come out. I'm just not sure what the best way is to release that information to you."

"I can keep your identity anonymous," I said.

"It's not me. It's my girlfriend. I'm trying to get her to speak to you. But she's reluctant to get involved. But enough time has gone by. Somebody should know about this information."

"What's it about?"

"It's about what was going on with Maura before she disappeared."

"Can you be more specific?"

"I'm sorry," he said. "You're on the right track. I just wanted to talk to you and make sure you were legitimate. I'll try to get her to talk. It's really hard for her, though. I'll try." He hung up.

I wondered who this man might be. Was he the boyfriend of

one of Maura's friends? I got the feeling he was being sincere. He didn't sound crazy, not like the psychics who sometimes called telling me about visions of Maura being held against her will in a drug den.

All I could do was hope his girlfriend would call back.

TWENTY

The Chief's Demons

I returned to Hanson in late July. I brought a digital printer with me and spent an afternoon in the library of Maura's high school, scanning pictures from yearbooks. Maura was quoted often in pages dedicated to cross-country.

"Work hard. Train early, before the season begins," she recommended to incoming freshmen, a simple quote under her grinning photograph. "Keep a constant positive attitude and remember to always appreciate your team members."

"We finally beat D-Y [Dennis-Yarmouth, Whitman-Hanson's rival], yet did not make the state meet," she said on another page. "With a little more hard work, combined with a lot less cutting practice and next year's outstanding crop of freshmen, W-H Cross Country should rise not only to league champs but also state."

When I was done, I drove up 93 to the Kancamagus Highway and then west past the accident site, into Haverhill. I met with Police Chief Byron Charles, who had been behind that desk for about six months. Charles had personally handled the search warrant of Maura's car, but he wouldn't speak much about the case since it was still an open investigation.

I pressed him on what the search of the vehicle revealed. He told me that, along with the spilled wine, they had also found a bottle of vodka and Kahlúa (Maura's favorite mixed drink was the Black Russian).

"What do you think happened to her?" I asked.

Charles shook his head. "Seven years is a long time to be hiding," he said. "I don't know. I think, my best guess . . . I really don't know. Nobody's heard from her in seven years. That's all I know. You should talk to Chief Williams. The former chief, I mean. The guy who was in charge when Maura disappeared."

On the way to Williams's house, I dropped by Cecil Smith's place. Smith was the first cop on the scene the night of Maura's accident. I found him in his front yard, tinkering with a mound of dirt beneath a radar dish. Smith had figured out how to build a green-energy generator to warm the water in his house using the captured radiant heat from rotting wood. He was a friendly fellow, anxious to bend my ear about the benefits of compost power. Eventually, we got around to talking about the accident.

"I don't drink," he said. "But I know what alcohol smells like, and the car smelled like alcohol. I could see it spilled all over the ceiling."

Smith had his own theory about what brought Maura up to New Hampshire.

"It was her scumbag boyfriend that made her want to drive up here," he said. "He came out in the news and was all, 'We loved her.' Well, fuck you. He was cheating on her. If it was a suicide, it was because of what he was doing to her. But if it was a suicide, where's the body? Why drive all the way up here just to kill yourself?"

Then he said with a weird smile, "You should really talk to Chief Williams."

I found Jeffrey Williams's house on Bradley Hill Road, a half mile up the mountain from where Maura got in her wreck. In front of his mansion is a big barn and on top of the barn is a golden calf weather vane. Something about the look of the place raised my hackles. I parked my car, walked to the front door, and knocked. Williams was already there and opened the door immediately. He's a large man with a long scar eating up his right cheek.

"What?"

"I'm a journalist working on—"

Williams slammed the door in my face.

I returned to my car, took out a notebook, and wrote down my contact info, along with a better explanation about what I was doing. Before I could take it back to the house, he opened the door and shouted at me. "Get off my property before I kick your ass!"

When I got back to my hotel room, I Googled the former chief and got a sense of why he was so aggressive toward reporters.

Williams had been a police officer in Haverhill for most of his fifteen years on the force and made chief in 2001. Things started to go bad for him in 2009, when he crashed his Harley. It was a severe accident that resulted in several surgeries. Three months later, he attempted to flee from police while driving drunk in Woodsville. The press ran his photo in the paper. He resigned. The officer who pulled him over? Cecil Smith.

Williams was not the only one who threatened to kick my ass that day.

TWENTY-ONE

What the TV Guy Told Me

In this part of New Hampshire, everyone pitches in. It's the frontier still, even with the new Wal-Mart. If you have a truck, you own a plow, and when it snows you go and dig out your neighbor and you don't charge for it. People check up on each other. Most everyone owns a police scanner. And everyone seems to have a small business on the side: towing, compost energy, weed.

I wasn't surprised to learn that the local TV repairman was also part-time EMS. Dick Guy, "the TV Guy," works out of a shop just behind the diner, where he fixes tube televisions. I wanted to speak to him because of this note I found in a police report: "Dick Guy mentioned that he had noticed a couple of odd things at the MVA [motor vehicle accident] that he is curious if HPD [Haverhill police department] was made aware of."

I found him at work. He was anxious to talk.

"Everything about the scene of the accident was weird," he said. "If she had just lost control of the car coming around that corner, she would have impacted the side of the curve. She didn't. What really happened was she clipped the corner on her left. She sheared the snowbank clean off and continued on to the other side, where it turned the car around."

Guy then drew a freehand map of what he saw that night, showing the sheared-off corner.

"To me, I'd say her car had stalled and she was trying to regain control as she came to the turn."

The accident had not happened as it was reported in the papers. Guy's version explained the inconsistent damage to the Saturn, the way the hood had smushed down on the driver's side. Clipping the corner could have done that.

I returned to the crash site to review the physics of the situation. Yes—it could have happened like the TV Guy said. Again, I'm no expert, but it looked good. And the TV Guy had seen plenty of accidents as volunteer EMS, enough for him to believe that the accepted explanation of the accident didn't make any sense.

While I was there, I walked to the house across from the weathered barn and spoke to Faith Westman. She'd become a character in the legend of Maura Murray's disappearance because she was the last one to see Maura before she vanished, watching her off and on from her window. After hearing the crash, Faith called 911. It was that call that placed an exact time on the accident, actually—7:27 P.M. According to the 911 log, she told the dispatcher that she saw a man sitting inside Maura's car, smoking a cigarette that night.

Faith was skittish and didn't want to talk about it. She didn't like how there were always people stopping by around the anniversary. But eventually, she opened up to me, to set the record straight.

"I heard a crash and then I went to the window," she said. "I saw the car. There was a red light in the car, which I thought might be the light from the end of a cigarette," said Westman. "But I never saw a man and the red light could have been anything. Maybe a cell phone light as she was trying to find a signal to call someone."

Another person who had a good view of the crash that night was John Marrotte, who lived across from Butch Atwood. I found him at home.

"I saw her get out and walk around the car," he told me. "When I looked out again, the police were there. She was gone. I don't know what happened. Only man who knows is up there." He pointed to the sky.

There's a shallow dirt lane that trails into the woods behind the scene of the accident. An old hermit lives back there. I checked with him. But his cabin was too far away to see anything that night.

I had hoped to speak to Rick Forcier, too. He was the man who lived at the corner of Wild Ammonoosuc and Bradley Hill, the guy who came forward months later with a story about seeing a jogger the night Maura vanished. But Forcier had moved away.

I stopped at the Swiftwater Stage Shop, a mile back toward Woodsville. The grocery and gas shop is run by Bill and Winnie. Bill, a medium-sized guy with a mostly bald head, was behind the register that day.

"Do you know how I can reach Rick Forcier?" I asked.

"No," said Bill. "And I'm not telling you a damn thing."

I was taken aback. I hadn't even introduced myself. "Why?" I asked.

"Because I'm tired of answering questions about that girl. And you're trying to make a buck."

"I'm not—"

"Get out of my store or I'm going to beat your head in."

This should have been enough motivation for me to leave. But can I be honest here? I'm the kind of guy who, when you tell me you're going to beat my head in, I'll stay around to make you do it. I've got a real self-destructive streak, especially when I'm angry. It's not something I'm proud of, but I'm telling you this because I'm trying to paint the scene. Here was a guy with information that might be helpful to me, information that might be helpful to finding out what really happened to Maura Murray, and instead he wanted to act tough and try to scare me. So what I did was I smiled and I said, kind of laughing, "Why are you so angry, man?"

"That's it," said Bill. He reached under the counter, grabbed a long wooden rod, and came at me. I didn't budge. I didn't think he'd really do it. And if he did, he'd give me a hell of a story. He grabbed me by the shirt and pushed me out of his shop.

"Maybe we should call the cops," I suggested. "Maybe they'd like to know why a guy who works a mile from where Maura went missing gets so upset when someone comes by asking questions about her."

He swung the bat up, and I really did think he was going to lay me out for a second. He seemed to think better of it, though, as two bikers were watching us from under an umbrella in the parking lot. He turned and walked back inside.

After I calmed down, I felt a little bad for the guy. He has a business to run, after all. And it probably does get old, the endless questions about the woman who vanished down the road, especially when the woman's father often tells reporters how he's convinced that some "local dirtbag" kidnapped her.

Bill is no dirtbag. Neither is Forcier. Though I never spoke to Forcier directly—he's not interested in talking about the case anymore—I've seen his low-budget, cringe-worthy music videos on YouTube. He's a goofball. I've spoken to a number of his friends and family and the picture they paint is of a folksy musician, prone to exaggeration, always wanting to tell a better story than the next guy. That's what I believe his sighting was. Just a story that got out of hand. Whoever he saw jogging that night, if he saw anyone at all, was almost certainly not Maura Murray.

Before I left New Hampshire, I drove out to Troop F's barracks over in Twin Mountain. The officers of Troop F protect and serve the citizens of Coos and Grafton counties and also the people who visit the White Mountain National Forest. Their jurisdiction covers three thousand square miles, but their office is no bigger than a Sizzler. Seven years after Maura's disappearance, her Saturn was still sitting in their evidence lot, out by the Dumpsters.

The car didn't look so bad. Its left front end was crumpled where it must have hit the corner of the turn (if the TV Guy's interpretation was accurate). The windshield was cracked on the driver's side. But the car was far from totaled. I had driven worse in college.

I took some pictures. Tried the door handle—locked. Peered in the windows. There were a few things worth reporting. First of all, I could see the red stain in the ceiling upholstery. Wine? I noticed a pen from First Citizens Bank resting on a seat, a parking permit with the picture of a green tree, an empty food container from a grocery store, a Stop & Shop loyalty card. There was also a tag or sticker from a pizza place called the Lynwood Café.

TWENTY-TWO

Aunt Janis

The Murrays were not interested in being interviewed for the book, so I tried the other side, the Mehrmans. Maura's mother—maiden name: Laurie Mehrman—died on May 4, 2009, Maura's twenty-seventh birthday. I used her obit to find Laurie's sister, Janis, who lived in Weymouth, where they had grown up.

Weymouth is a blue-collar burg with a view of the Boston skyline. It's an old town, the second-oldest European settlement, in fact, founded in 1622 by the guy who started Plymouth. Only, things didn't go so well in Weymouth. The colonists hadn't accounted for the harsh winter and when supplies ran out, they stole from the Indians. Things got nasty. Myles Standish tried to mediate things. When that didn't work, they just murdered the local chiefs. Lots of blood spilled here.

This was where Fred met Laurie.

I found Janis at home, and she invited me in for a glass of wine. She was nervous and overly chatty, but quite welcoming. We sat on floral-patterned sofas and spoke about Maura, whose pictures were placed throughout the room.

"Every spring break, every summer, Maura would come here," said Janis. "Christmas, Thanksgiving, she was here."

Maura was a very shy young woman, but she also had a temper, Janis said. Though she didn't get angry easily. Maura kept her emotions bottled up inside, but when it got to be too much, hoo boy. Look out.

Maura's grandmother, Ruth, 91 years young, was downstairs, and we spoke quietly so she wouldn't hear. Ruth, who was very close to Maura, never talked about the disappearance. About her sister Laurie, all Janis offered was that she was "an excellent mother . . . when the kids were little."

Janis always thought Fred was "a very odd duck." He met Laurie at a Weymouth park one day, she said. He spotted her playing baseball and then introduced himself. He was in college. Laurie was just fifteen. "He pursued her until she went out with him."

The marriage fell apart when Laurie got pregnant with Kurt, said Janis. Fred was not Kurt's father. Kurt's dad was a man named Kevin Noble. In 1994, Noble was convicted of murdering his own brother after an argument over a loud radio turned physical.

After the affair, Fred moved back to Weymouth, but he returned to Hanson daily to condition his daughters, training them to be champion runners. Maura's little brother went by "Kurt Noble Murray" and maintained a cordial relationship with Fred all his life. Sometimes Fred even took him to the White Mountains with Maura. Fred took his girls hiking a lot.

"They vacationed up there all the time," said Janis. The Jigger Johnson camp, on the Kancamagus Highway, was their favorite spot. She shook her head as she thought back on it. "I always thought that was strange, Maura going camping up there with her father. They would share a tent. She was, what, fourteen, fifteen, sixteen? If my dad had ever asked me to go camping alone with him and share a tent, I would have said, 'What are you, nuts?'"

Senator Ted Kennedy nominated Maura for West Point, said Janis (prospective cadets must appeal to high-ranking government officials to be accepted as a nominee). It was at West Point that Maura met "Mr. Nice Guy," as she calls Billy Rausch. "He cheated on her for years. One of her sister Julie's girlfriends. As if that wouldn't get back to her."

When they were younger, Julie and Maura were inseparable, but after she moved out of the house to attend West Point, Julie Murray's relationship with their mother deteriorated, said Janis— "Julie and Laurie didn't talk for a long time"—and things were not great between Julie and Maura, either. After Maura went missing, Julie traveled up to help with the search only once, as far as Janis knew.

"I've never been up there," Janis said, scrunching her nose. "I never want to go."

She recalled how Kurt, whom Maura doted on and protected, was afraid of what he might find in New Hampshire. "Kurt was scared of finding a body," she said. "He told me, 'I don't know what I'd ever do if I did find her.'"

Janis believed Maura went up to New Hampshire to get away from Fred. "They had an argument about that car accident," she said, meaning the late-night crash in Amherst that put Fred's Toyota in the shop. "He really reamed her over it. But he claims it wasn't why she left."

Janis thinks that after Maura got up there, someone took her.

She leaned forward and whispered, "My gut tells me the police had something to do with it."

*　*　*

I drove out to Fred's house in Weymouth that night, expecting to find him at last. On all the court documents, Fred's address is listed as 22 Walker Street. It's a simple, white two-story home. But the house was boarded up as if no one had lived there for some time.

It was almost dark and the place had a haunted look about it. So I left, promising to come back on my next trip to New England. During the day.

TWENTY-THREE

Baby Brother

Maura grew up in a modest split-level on Joanne Drive in Hanson. The road ends in a cul-de-sac where everyone kind of knows each other's business. It's one of those places where everyone waves as you drive by.

I knocked on the front door, but if anyone was home they didn't answer. I was supposed to meet Fred, Jr., the oldest of the Murray siblings, for breakfast. But he'd called at the last minute and said he'd changed his mind. At the time, Fred, Jr., was deep for trouble and didn't want to be around reporters. He'd been arrested for shoplifting Craftsman tools at a Sears. When the police walked him out of Sears to his vehicle to get his ID, they found three hypodermic needles under the floor mat.

Next door to the Murrays were the Carpenters. Maura's oldest sister, Kathleen, had married one of the Carpenter boys. But no one was home there, either.

I went across the street and visited Linda Higgins. She had

been friends with Laurie, Maura's mother. "We traded flowers," she said. "These are her irises by the mailbox."

The Murray family was always short on money, Linda explained. She did her best to send a little their way when she could, sometimes asking the Murray girls to babysit. Kathleen babysat for a while, but then the Higginses noticed someone had called a sex line during the hours Kathleen was watching the children. After that, Linda would only ask Maura to babysit.

She remembered Maura going door-to-door once selling Cutco knives to earn spending cash.

Laurie worried about Maura more than the other children, said Linda. "I remember Laurie saying, 'Maura's so smart. But she's not *street*-smart.'" Maura always wanted to believe the best of people.

I asked her how I might find Maura's other siblings. "Her younger brother Kurt works at Lowe's," she said. "He's probably there right now."

I found Kurt resting in his car at the back of the Lowe's parking lot. He was on break, listening to some tunes. A young man, dark hair, ripped, easy on the eyes. He didn't seem surprised to see me in such a strange location. He climbed out of the car and leaned against its frame as we talked.

Maura liked to play catch with him on the slow street outside their house, he recalled. Ground-ball drills. If he botched a play, she'd make him run laps.

"We went on adventures in the woods, too. She'd take me to the river tucked in back there. We used to go on camping trips. Jigger Johnson was our favorite spot. Sometimes she'd go with her father and I'd come along. Sometimes they just went themselves."

When Kurt was there, he and Maura would jump off bridges into the water. There was a rope swing at Jigger Johnson. Maura was fearless, he says. "She'd always put on a show. She'd jump off that rope swing and do all these twists in the air before diving into the water."

Maura took Kurt along with her to Shaw's when she shopped for the family's groceries. She turned the chore into a game, leaving items at the ends of aisles for Kurt to race to and then return to the cart. She taught him to bargain-shop. She tried to turn him into a runner, too.

"I hated running, so when she'd go running, I'd ride my bike along with her."

Kurt came home from school one day and the whole family was waiting in the living room. Maura was missing, they told him. Everyone packed up and drove to New Hampshire. They stayed at the Wells River Motel for a bit and then at a condo in Lincoln owned by Fred, Jr.'s boss. They were looking for Maura's body in the woods. But Kurt never believed she'd killed herself.

It made sense that Maura would have gone up there with the intention of clearing her mind, he said. "I think she needed a break. All this talk of suicide . . . why would she drive all the way up there to do it? Doesn't make sense. That place was special for us. I think she went up there to take a breather and then something happened."

When their mother got sick, Kurt moved back home and took care of Laurie until the end, dropping out of school so he could work during the day to pay their utilities. The kid's been through a lot more than his fair share, but he still has a quick smile and a laid-back disposition. I found him to be a little inspiring, to tell the truth.

I asked him where Maura's father was these days. He said Fred was living on the Cape, near Falmouth. He gave me Fred's cell number. I left a message that night but never heard back.

Later, Kurt friended me on Facebook, and that's how I discovered that in 2010 he'd written a song about his sister's disappearance. His lyrics suggest he and his siblings believe Maura deliberately ran away.

> *What have we done*
> *To make you turn your back on us and run. . . .*

Before I returned to Ohio, I dropped by Andrea Connolly's house in Rockland, five miles away. Andrea was one of Maura's close friends from high school, part of that inner circle of girls from Whitman-Hanson High. Andrea wasn't around, but her mother was. She invited me in, gave me a drink, and called her daughter. Andrea said that Fred had told her not to talk to me. But her mother was kind enough to tell me a few stories.

"Andrea could never go inside Maura's house," she said. "Maura would come out when you picked her up, before you got to the door. Wouldn't let anyone inside. She never drove. She never had enough money for a car."

Andrea's mother told me that about a year before the disappearance, Maura spent New Year's Eve at the house of a friend of the Connollys in Goshen, New Hampshire, just a bit south of Haverhill. When the girls learned about Maura's crash, they called the people who lived next door to the property in Goshen and had them check the house to see if Maura was there. She wasn't. Still, she said, the detectives seemed very interested in that particular bit of information.

I was, too. If Maura knew the place was empty in the winter, it would have been the perfect place to lay low for a while. And it would explain why, after searching for rentals, she apparently gave up without actually booking one.

TWENTY-FOUR

How an Abduction Happens

When I was thirteen, a man tried to abduct me. In a Hollywood screenplay this would be the scene the director uses to explain why I became a true crime journalist—my origin story, as it were. But my fascination with human predators actually began a couple years before this. By the time I was thirteen, I was already obsessing over Amy Mihaljevic: riding my bike to area shopping malls, looking for the face of her killer in the crowds. And before Amy, there was my grandfather, whom we'll get to soon.

This thing that happened when I was thirteen I don't talk about much. I give a dozen or so presentations about cold cases every year, mostly at local libraries. You'd think I'd use it as part of my shtick. But I don't. It's one of those stories that are hard to digest. People come to my talks to get scared. But a good storyteller knows that people need degrees of separation from true horror, and I think that separation is lost if I start talking about me and this thing that happened.

My parents divorced when I was four, and my father got custody of me. My mother picked me up for visitation every other weekend. In 1991, she was living in an apartment in Old Brooklyn, a suburb of Cleveland not far from the city zoo. Across the street was a section of the Metroparks, a part of the "Emerald Necklace" that wraps around Cuyahoga County. Nearby was the Memphis Kiddie Park, which had a carousel, baby rockets, and a short roller coaster called the Little Dipper. In between the park and the carnival was a railroad track.

I was thirteen and I liked to explore. I set off from my mother's apartment one Saturday morning, crossed the street to the park, and made my way toward a creek that runs between cobblestone retaining walls. At the end of the parking lot was a concrete bathroom, and as I passed the men's room doorway I noticed a tall man with dark hair standing just outside. He looked at me and fiddled with the crotch of his pants.

Kids, like adults, are quite capable of rationalizing dangerous behavior. *He must have an itch,* I thought. But then he began tugging and I knew something was *off* about this situation. Still, I kept walking. I started down a grassy path into the woods. I turned and saw that the man was walking after me.

I kept walking, willing myself not to panic. At a long, straight stretch of trail I turned again. The man was now about a hundred feet behind and walking briskly. I started to jog. I looked again. He was jogging now. And he looked angry. Angry that I was making him jog. For the first time I realized the danger I was in. There was nothing but more woods and the river this way. I couldn't get back to my mom. This man was blocking my escape. I began to run.

When I was thirteen, I was skinny as a rail, 120 pounds. I spent long days riding my bike over the backcountry hills around my father's house. And I was a runner. I was fast. But this guy was faster than me. Skinny, fit, he tore after me. All pretense was abandoned. I knew what he was now. And he knew that I knew. And that was that.

I saw the train tracks on my left. They led back to the apartments. It was a way out, maybe. I ran through the underbrush, tearing through skunk weed and berry bushes. In a moment I was on the tracks, running back toward the road, the white gravel between the ties kicking up behind my feet. The thin man was out of the woods now, too. He ran after me. It was clear that he would catch up to me long before I got to the road, before I got anywhere near the apartments. I looked for a way out. But the ground on either side had risen to sheer walls of rock, twenty feet high. A tight canyon.

There was one chance: to scale the wall. If I slipped, or if I was too slow, that was it, man. That was it.

I turned and dug my fingers into the rock and clay and pulled myself off the ground. I scrambled up as fast as I could. I didn't slip. In ten seconds, I was all the way up. I looked down. The man stood on the tracks directly below me, looking up with eyes full of hate. I gave him the finger and then ran back to my mother.

She called the rangers, but by the time they got there, he was long gone. The rangers told me to not come back to the park alone. "Those bathrooms are where the queers hang out," one of them said. This was long enough ago that Ohio cops still didn't differentiate between homosexuals and pedophiles.

I think about this day a lot. What had that man planned to do with me? How had he planned to keep me from screaming? Was he just going to fondle me and be on his way or did he have murder in mind? Did he have a knife on his belt? How many times had he done this before? Who was he? Would I ever see him again?

The thing that scares me the most is the way he looked at me in the end. Those eyes said it all. He was so angry. He was furious that I had managed to get away. Where did that hate come from? When did it start?

I don't think Maura Murray was abducted from the side of the road. I never did. Abductions are messy, like mine. Or they're organized, like Amy Mihaljevic's. And if they are organized, that means they were planned, meticulously.

Amy Mihaljevic was abducted across the street from the Bay Village police station, in broad daylight. Her abductor had groomed her for days, calling her at home, promising to take her shopping to get a gift for her mother if she'd just meet him at the plaza. She waited for her abductor and went willingly with him.

My attempted abduction had been messy because it wasn't planned. I had run for several minutes and then escaped. Any number of people could have happened by to see me running away from that man.

The one thing I know for sure about Maura's accident on Wild Ammonoosuc Road was that it wasn't planned. No way was it staged—not the dangerous way it occurred; not in front of several homes, full of potential witnesses. The impact was hard enough to deploy the air bags and really could have injured her. It wasn't planned. And if it wasn't planned, an abduction from the scene could not have been organized. It would have been messy, like mine. But she disappeared, and no one saw it happen. There were no signs of a struggle.

No, this was no abduction.

I was beginning to form a theory to explain Maura's vanishing act. There was another way it could have happened: She could have been traveling in tandem with another driver. The other driver would be ahead of her, leading the way east. After the accident, the second driver turned around and picked her up. If she knew the driver, it would have taken only a second for Maura to get in the vehicle and tell the driver to take off. That would explain why no one saw it happen—it was too quick. If someone forced Maura into a car, she would have screamed, alerting the neighbors. She would have fought back. She was not weak. She was a goddamn West Point cadet. A tandem driver explained everything. But if that's what happened, who was driving the other car?

TWENTY-FIVE

A Lucky Break

On August 14, 2011, Akron was hit by a once-in-a-century downpour and sometime during that storm the front wall of my basement collapsed. That's where I keep my books, my notes, and my writing. I was able to salvage the important stuff. My insurance wouldn't cover a dime because it was flood damage (*hydrostatic pressure:* the two most evil words in the English language), and I was looking at fifteen grand in repairs. It could have been tragic, like move-back-home-with-your-parents tragic, except that I'd just received the advance on my first novel that week, a book I'd finished after I was fired from *Cleveland Scene* as a way to keep my mind busy. The novel told the story of a young man who worked for an alt-weekly and the odd crime he became obsessed with ("Write what you know"). *The Man from Primrose Lane* saved my house. There are no accidents; I've come to believe this. For the next six weeks, all my energy was spent rebuilding the cottage. There was no time to delve into the Maura Murray case. But while I was away, my Baker Street Irregulars were hard at work trying to make sense of the items I'd discovered in Maura's abandoned car.

A reader named Chris sent me an e-mail, explaining that it wouldn't be weird for a young woman from Hanson to have a magnet from the Lynwood Café in her car. "It is absolutely Famous in eastern MA and throughout New England for its unique Pizza," he wrote. "People come from 75+ mile radius to eat there or get takeout. Its sort of an old looking 4-way stop but its not 'sketchy' and does not attract weirdos or anything like that. Considering the new demographics of Randolph, its probably one of the safer areas of town due to it being on the Holbrook line."

An ambitious sleuth named Samantha grabbed the account number from Maura's Stop & Shop card and ran it through the company's Web site. "I was interested in seeing if I could pull up a list of items purchased under that number," she wrote. "I could enter the card number, which was associated with Maura's name, but it requested I register an online account to view any information. I did not feel comfortable doing that. However, the site automatically filled in fields for the registration form—I'm assuming based off of what Maura provided when she set up the account. It included the phone number and address for Fred's house in Weymouth—and the e-mail address: aasic@aol.com."

The most promising lead turned out to be that pen from Citizens Bank. A woman named Stef e-mailed: "In 2007 I worked as a teller for a bank that has branches in NY, PA, and New England. It would get pretty boring sometimes, and I am nosy, so during lulls I would go through the database and search for people I knew, famous people, random missing people, etc. One time I searched 'Maura Murray.' As of the end of 2006/early 2007, there was a Maura Murray, born May 4, 1982, with an active account opened in New Hampshire. If I recall correctly, it was attached to a car loan, and the account was active in that it was collecting payments."

When I wrote back, she confirmed it was Citizens Bank that she worked for, adding: "Citizens Bank no longer does car loans, but they did then. To have one, you needed a checking account that was attached to the car loan. By 'active,' that meant there had been payments within the last 30–60 days on the car loan, because once a person was late and sent to collections, the account would read 0000 next to the name and be flagged. I just remember thinking it seemed strange it was a Maura Murray with the same date of birth and the loan was opened in NH, since that is where she had disappeared from."

Of course, these answers only led to more questions.

After the bulldozers left, I reached out to Maura's college friends: Sara Alfieri and Kate Markopoulos. But Sara and Kate were obstinately silent. I tried Kate's childhood home and got her father. "She really should talk to you," he said. He promised to have her call.

I found a list of Maura's UMass teammates online, and the first person who replied to my messages was a woman named Nastaran Shams. That's pronounced "Nast-ron" in New English, by the way, but she goes by "Nast." Nast majored in psychology and microbiology at UMass and was also a multi-eventer for the track team.

"Maura was shy but extremely ambitious," Nast told me one night over the phone. "She was just wonderful. Everyone who knew her loved her."

Maura's reputation preceded her, literally. Nast heard rumors about this big-deal runner chick who was transferring from West Point. And she was gorgeous to boot. But when Maura finally arrived, she carried no ego. Nast did the introductions and invited her to a party. Soon, Maura was friends with everyone on the team, and particularly close with Kate Markopoulos.

At the time, the young women on the track team liked to crash at a beat-up apartment off-campus, where they could drink and not worry about getting caught. When you're a member of a collegiate track team, especially at a number-one party school like the Zoo, you become extremely close to your teammates. You eat with them. You condition with them every day. You hang out with them after practice. As Nast explained, "Sports in college is a kind of cult."

Maura introduced her new friends to her beau, Billy Rausch. They hated him from the start and plotted ways to break them up—especially when Maura told them that he'd cheated on her. "Let's just say we weren't the biggest fans of that dude." Of course, it wasn't difficult to find men interested in hooking up with Maura.

"A bunch of guys had crushes on her," said Nast. "She was an incredible runner. She was in incredible shape. She was extremely kind. And she was willing to go out and have a little fun."

But Maura's demeanor suddenly changed the winter before she disappeared. "I was told she'd been injured," Nast said. "Then, I was told she was sick. We were gearing up for spring track and she wasn't there. This was going into our senior year."

After Maura went missing, nobody told the track team for a while. Nast heard a rumor that something bad had happened but didn't know what. Kate had vanished, too; she'd stopped coming to practice. About a week later, they were told that Maura had disappeared in New Hampshire. Investigators showed up at practice. "Don't mind them," the coach said. "Just answer their questions, truthfully."

"We didn't see Kate at all," said Nast. "I don't know if she took a leave of absence or what. But Kate really closed up after that. She disappeared for a while. When she came back she'd lost all this weight. She kicked butt. She must have taken it out on the track." Kate never talked about Maura again.

"All our lives would have been a little different if this hadn't happened," said Nast, who coaches track now. "Some of us have become more spiritual because of it. You either open up or you close up."

I asked her if anything ever came of the men she tried to set Maura up with.

"Well," she said. "There was this one. Hossein Baghdadi. He was our assistant track coach. Volunteer grad student. He had an interest in Maura. She had an interest in him. I'm pretty sure he and Kate and Maura hung out. But I think Maura wanted to keep that secret. Every time we were together and Hoss was there, they were really comfortable with each other. That indicated to me that they also hung out together outside of our group. But Hoss wanted to keep his position with the team. So it wasn't something that could happen in the open."

Crystal Therrien was Maura's team captain at UMass. She said Hoss was not as nice as he let on. "He was very intense. He had a really cocky way about him," she said. "He was not a very good leader. We'd be running hills and he'd try to motivate us by yelling, 'Suck it up!' I mean, *yelling*. That works for some people. But not me."

It struck me how the people I'd spoken to in Hanson had described Fred in almost exactly the same words.

I tracked Hossein down pretty quickly, a name like that. I thought that even if there was any truth to Nast's hunch, he was sure to deny the relationship or gloss over the prurient details.

"Yes," he said. "We slept together. But you have to know something. Maura Murray was a very promiscuous woman. I wasn't the only guy on that team she had sex with."

TWENTY-SIX

Maura's Lovers

Hoss is an attractive dude: olive-skinned, insouciant stubble, long-limbed and slim; a marathon runner. Over the phone, his voice was clipped and rushed, like he couldn't wait to get to the finish line of our interview. We spoke only that once, long distance, me outside an Akron bar, him somewhere in the Pacific Northwest. But that short conversation was enough to get a better picture of Maura than a hundred articles written about her disappearance would have provided.

"We hung out at the end of the semester, in 2003," he said. "Then she went home for the summer. She came back to Amherst once, in June, to visit me. We were in constant contact and then she just kind of fell off the face of the earth. I got this random e-mail about her boyfriend. They had started things back up. She left whatever we had."

He got to know Maura well in those weeks. Enough to know

that she came from a troubled family. "Maura didn't get along with her mother," he said. "She was angry with her mom. They had a falling-out. And she never mentioned her father. Not once. I never even knew her father was still alive."

She didn't have much respect for Billy, he said. "Billy wanted her to be in certain places at certain times so he could check up on her. He could be demanding. That's just my impression. He seemed to be very chauvinistic."

She and Hoss had a lot of fun while keeping the relationship on the down-low—watching movies at his house late at night, eating out. They planned to go camping in the White Mountains. Hoss knew the area well; he often went fly-fishing up there.

Lying in bed with Hoss, Maura sometimes talked about running away. "She said, 'I wish I could disappear,' but she never said how she would do it. I always thought Mexico."

A few months before she really did disappear, he met Maura for lunch. "That was the last time I saw her," he said. "I thought we could at least be friends."

After Hoss got wind that Maura was missing, he spoke to a UMass detective, but it wasn't clear to me that they ever discussed the sexual relationship. He wasn't the only one, he kept reminding me. Maura dated other men on the team. Someone named Dave, he said; some guy called "Scrub."

Baghdadi wasn't lying.

I spoke to three men who ran with Maura at UMass. Each told me a slightly different version of the same story. One had first-hand knowledge. The gist was this: In 2003, Maura and a close friend were invited to after-hours parties at the athletic pool with three select upperclassmen (who have gone on to become prominent businessmen). One of the guys had keys to the facility and they would all sneak into the pool late at night and drink. And swim. And have sex.

According to each of my sources, these pool parties were straight-up orgies. Maura had sex with all three men. In one night. One after the other.

"It's not a big deal," said one. "It was college. It was college hedonistic stuff."

Only one of the men involved in the gang bang ever spoke to police, after his ex-girlfriend suggested to local detectives that he might be involved with Maura's disappearance. But he swears he never spoke to Maura again after she left the team.

TWENTY-SEVEN

BFF

If anyone had insight into where Maura was heading the night she disappeared, it was Kate Markopoulos, Maura's best friend at UMass. But ever since Maura went missing, Kate has kept mum. She was quoted only once, in early newspaper accounts, and gave no useful information. When asked about her best friend, she kept it vague: "She took care of stuff on her own. That's Maura." She was never actively involved in the searches for her friend. After weeks of my trying to contact her, Kate finally called me one evening.

Kate provided a lot of inconsequential details. She and Maura liked watching *Bottle Rocket,* a movie about a couple of friends who steal some money and then go into hiding until they're caught by police. They often went shopping together. She said that Fred was a nice guy.

"You could tell he loved her to bits," she said. "She loved him. She talked about him all the time." She knew that Maura and her dad would often go to the White Mountain area of New Hampshire together. They would go away for days sometimes.

Maura was planning to move to Oklahoma to be with Billy, she said. "But she wasn't thrilled about moving. It was the middle of nowhere. She was going to get a job at a hospital; she was going to move because she loved him."

What did Kate remember about the Saturday that Fred came to visit, the weekend before Maura disappeared? In newspaper and television interviews, Fred had stated that he was in Amherst that weekend with $4,000 in cash to help Maura look for a car. But Kate said neither Fred nor Maura mentioned car shopping that night.

After they dropped Fred off at his hotel, she and Maura returned to Kennedy Hall to party it up in Sara Alfieri's dorm room, she said. "It was an even mix of men and women; pretty squished in there. I left around two, two thirty. One guy offered to walk me back to my place. Maura said she was going to bed. I didn't know she was getting back into the car. That was the last time I saw her."

In hindsight, Kate wondered if Maura might have been stressed about nursing school. Maybe it got to be too much and she left just to get away for a while, and then something else happened.

"The more I think about it, the more I realize I didn't really know her," she said.

Kate claimed she didn't know about Maura's fling with Hoss, even though Kate was sometimes the third wheel when the two got together outside practice.

The more Kate talked the more I got the feeling she was being deceptive. It was in her hesitant and measured answers. The careful wording. It felt to me that she was being overly cautious with her responses, and I did not understand why.

The detectives felt that way about Kate, too. Some got very

angry with her and her faulty memory. "There were good cops and bad cops," she recalled. "They kept saying, 'What do you mean you don't know who else was at the party?' They couldn't understand why I couldn't remember."

Neither could I. As Kate described it, Sara's room was packed. A man who was there walked Kate back to her room. But afterward she couldn't identify a single person other than Sara. And when pressed for specific things that happened during the party in the hours that she was there with Maura, her memory goes blank again: She doesn't remember anything.

It was hard to reach Kate for follow-up questions. She worked odd hours at a bar in Saratoga Springs. After I sent an e-mail asking her again about the other people who may have been at the party that night, she wrote: "I understand it would be helpful if I could remember names but it is just not happening. It was long ago and I barely knew those people nor would I see some of them again."

That last sentence is hinky. "Nor would I see some of them again?" Which of them *did* she see again?

After this awkward conversation, I placed Kate at the top of my short list of possibilities for the tandem driver. Hoss was on there, too. And Fred, for that matter. Nothing Kate told me made much sense.

It wasn't until much later that I learned that Kate Markopoulos had a very good reason to avoid police and reporters.

TWENTY-EIGHT

Consider the Red Herring

There's a clue I haven't mentioned yet. It might be the most important clue in the whole case. Or it might be a red herring. I don't know. The only thing I'm sure of is that it's goddamn peculiar. The guy who towed Maura's Saturn away from the scene of the accident in Haverhill found a rag stuffed into the tailpipe.

Mike Lavoie (say it, "La-voy") was vegging on his couch when he got the call about the accident. He's a likeable storyteller with a thick mustache and a goofy grin, the sort of guy who likes to razz his employees. But he doesn't joke about Maura Murray. He was kind of sick of people asking questions about her by the time I found him. But after he cooled down, he told me how he jumped into his truck pretty quickly after the call that night and drove out to Wild Ammonoosuc Road.

He towed Maura's car back to his place. The police told him to keep the Saturn in his garage—not his shop garage, but the garage at his house—under lock and key, until they could move it to the Troop F barracks. Lavoie noticed the rag in the tailpipe and pointed it out to Fred Murray when he came by to look at the Saturn a couple days after his daughter disappeared.

Fred explained that it was a rag he'd recently given to Maura to keep in her trunk. "He said that he told Maura to put it in the tailpipe to keep it from smoking. The car was not running well."

Something about that statement did not ring true to me. I've driven some junk cars, and my father-in-law runs a body shop. I've never heard of someone blocking a tailpipe to keep it from smoking. I'm no expert, but I'm not real sure you'd want to do that. Plugging a tailpipe is a good way to make a car stall.

Detective Scarinza was equally befuddled by this bit of information. "I don't understand that one at all," he said. "That rag . . . Is it an attempt to kill yourself? Because it's not going to work. But why the hell else would someone stick a rag up their tailpipe? It's an anomaly."

Dick Guy, the TV Guy, believes the rag is paramount. "There's only two explanations for the rag in the tailpipe," he said, his voice low, conspiratorial. "One: Someone stuffed it in there to get her to stall. Two: Someone put it in there after the accident to muddy the waters."

"Muddy the waters." That's what a red herring does. In literature, a red herring is a device the author uses to mislead the reader, casting suspicion on a character to shield the identity of the true killer a bit longer. Linguists disagree on the origin of this expression, but it probably came from a sneaky trick criminals adopted to fuck with tracking hounds hundreds of years ago. A "red" herring is a herring that has been cured in brine, making it particularly smelly. A journalist in the 1800s claimed you could drag red herrings away from your trail to divert any hounds that were tracking you. But who would want to mislead police in Maura's case? Her killer? Maybe. If you believe she was murdered. Maura herself? Someone who knows why she was in New Hampshire to begin with? How about someone who knows his fingerprints will be on the rag if it is ever tested?

Red herring or not, the rag in the tailpipe is fishy.

Let's devour at least one more red herring while we're at it.

Several news outlets reported that Maura called Billy a couple days after she disappeared. As Billy was traveling from Fort Sill to New Hampshire to join the search, Billy shut off his cell phone while walking through the Dallas/Fort Worth airport. There was a strange message when he switched it back on. Billy's mother, Sharon, described the message to the *Whitman-Hanson Express*: "It was very short—consisted of a shivering, soft whimpering sound with labored breathing, as if someone was very cold."

Billy, of course, tried to call back. He found that the call was made using a prepaid card that could not be traced. Sharon had purchased two AT&T calling cards and given them to Maura during the holidays.

Did Maura use one of these cards to call Billy? Was she lost somewhere, trapped in the cold, dying of hypothermia?

In online message boards, a lot of importance was given to this phone call early on. After all, it proves that Maura was alive for days after she vanished.

The thing about police investigations that can be frustrating for armchair sleuths is that detectives have no obligation to share information with the public. They tracked this clue down in the first month of the investigation.

"It was a Red Cross worker trying to reach out to Billy," explained Scarinza. Red Cross officials act as liaisons to get emergency leave for enlisted soldiers. The caller didn't want to leave a message, hoping to speak to Billy directly. "I verified that phone call. It's verified. We spoke to the caller from the Red Cross."

TWENTY-NINE

The Londonderry Ping

Scouring the Web one day, I found an obscure site, Chris King's First Amendment Page, which had published some information related to Maura's disappearance. According to his Blogspot profile, King once worked for the attorney general's office. He had a background in journalism, though he listed his current occupation as "Metaphysical Reductionist," whatever that may be. Most of the blog was devoted to ridiculing law enforcement officials. But sometimes King investigated local crimes. While combing through documents related to Fred's civil suit against the state, King found a search warrant that someone had mistakenly left in the public file.

Here is the text of the warrant as it was published on King's site:

Supporting Affidavit for Issuance of Search Warrant I, Todd D. Landry, do hereby depose and say;

1. That I am currently employed by the State Police and have been for the past ten years. Currently, I am assigned as a Detective at Troop-F in Twin Mountain, NH. I have received extensive training in the investigation of criminal matters.

2. That on February 9, 2004 at 1927 hours the Haverhill, NH Police Department responded to a single vehicle motor vehicle crash on Route 112 in Haverhill, NH. Upon arrival, Sgt. Cecil Smith was unable to locate the driver of the vehicle. Subsequent investigation determined that the driver of the vehicle was MAURA MURRAY (d.o.b. 05/04/82), 22 Walker Street, Weymouth, MA.

3. A witness at the scene later confirmed that the driver was MURRAY.

4. An extensive search of the area has been conducted and MURRAY has not been located.

5. During the course of this investigation, Cellular Telephone records have been obtained by Law Enforcement that were used by MURRAY. A representative from Sprint Corporate Security advised this affiant that during the late afternoon hours of February 9, 2004, an outgoing telephone call was made to Murray from the Londonderry, NH Sprint tower. This call had to have been made from within a 22-mile radius of the tower. The identity of this caller and telephone number has not been made as of this date.

6. That identifying the caller of the telephone call could
   be pertinent to the ongoing investigation and may
   lead to the whereabouts of Maura Murray.

Todd D. Landry

Londonderry is a town way the hell on the eastern side of
New Hampshire, just north of Massachusetts, off Route 93.

I asked Lieutenant Landry if the search warrant was legit.
Here's what he wrote back:

> *Mr. Renner,*
> *In response to your questions I offer the following:*
> *The investigation is and has been on-going since the*
> *night Maura Murray went missing. In order to protect*
> *the integrity of the investigation I am limited to what can*
> *be released. In conferring with the lead prosecutor that is*
> *overseeing the case I can only confirm that the first respond-*
> *ing police officer that was on the scene was Sgt. Cecil Smith*
> *of the Haverhill Police Department.*
> *Thank You for your understanding in this matter.*
> *Respectfully, Lt. Todd Landry*

So is the warrant real? I think so. King, when contacted,
stood by it. Also, it's too esoteric to be made up. As a journalist I
know that sometimes records that should not be made public are
accidentally left in public files. While researching the terrible
crimes of Akron serial killer Bob Buell, I once found secret grand
jury testimony.

If the warrant is legit, it means that someone called Maura
from eastern New Hampshire shortly before she disappeared. Was

it someone traveling up Route 93 from Massachusetts? The Kancamagus Highway, the road where Maura disappeared, is the main
connector between Route 91 out of Amherst and Route 93 out of
Boston. Was someone coming up the other side of the state to
meet her in the middle? Was this my tandem driver?

THIRTY

The Man with the Knife

Early on, a man named Larry Moulton claimed that his brother, Claude, killed Maura. He gave Fred Murray a knife he said was used in the crime. Fred used this evidence to support his "local dirtbag" theory and shipped it to the police to be tested for DNA. Larry died a few years later. Cancer.

One of my Irregulars dug into Larry's story and uncovered an interesting bit of family history. A woman named Jean Caccavaro disappeared from the side of Wild Ammonoosuc Road back in 1977, not far from the site of Maura's accident. Jean was very similar to Maura in appearance. And a year after Jean vanished, Claude Moulton married Jean's daughter.

I immediately reached out to Larry's surviving family to learn what I could about the Moulton brothers. At the time of Maura's disappearance in 2004, Claude was living with a woman he had started dating when she was fourteen and he was thirty-four. They started sleeping together when she turned seventeen, she said.

They lived in an A-frame house on Valley Road about a mile from where Maura was last seen—the same house to which Fred's private investigators had taken cadaver dogs. One of the dogs had hit on a spot in the closet there. Days after Larry handed over the knife, Claude scrapped his red Volvo.

After Larry went to the Murrays with the knife, Claude told family members that Larry had made up the story in order to get the reward money being offered for information about Maura's disappearance. Larry had a history of drug use and was not an altogether likable guy.

The Haverhill police took the tip seriously enough that they asked Claude to sit for a lie detector test, confirmed to me by several sources. But nothing ever came of it and Claude doesn't appear to be a suspect any longer.

After I posted about Claude's link to Jean Caccavaro's family and the odd similarities between that woman's disappearance and Maura's, I got a call from Jean's ex-husband, James. He's up in years now. Retired. Cantankerous.

"Guess what?" he said. "Jean's alive and well. How's that for you?"

For years, James Caccavaro was treated like a murderer by New Hampshire police, the prime suspect in his wife's 1977 disappearance. But that changed when she returned from the dead in 1984. Jean had simply run away from her family to start a new life. He knows what it's like to be the center of suspicion, and even though Claude is no longer with his daughter, James feels for the man in a way probably nobody else can.

THIRTY-ONE

22 Walker

Like the Amy Mihaljevic case before, my investigation into the disappearance of Maura Murray was edging away from academic curiosity and into the realm of obsession. I thought about her disappearance all the time, working the clues around to fit them together into a logical narrative—the rag in the tailpipe, Maura's breakdown at work, the Londonderry ping. The mystery was maddening. Enticingly so.

I felt the pull of the North Country every day. I wanted to go back. I wanted to walk around the places she had been.

In late October, I returned to Weymouth. That's where Fred's house was. 22 Walker. Maura had used that address for mail, too, even though she had lived with her mother in Hanson.

Walker Street is a nub of a road and you can only go out the way you came in. Years ago, Fred's father built the houses on Walker for his family, and some of the extended Murrays still lived there. Fred's place was in foreclosure. Unpaid taxes.

I walked around the side of the old house. Some of the windows were boarded. A rectangle of plywood was nailed across the side door and someone had come along and pried up the bottom. I looked into the kitchen. Opened cans of dog food were piled on the floor, reaching to the sink. Empty Coors boxes were stacked in large mounds, four feet high. Out back, the remnants of a shed where Fred's brother had lived, according to neighbors, leaned against itself. Under planks of wood I found a bunch of mail addressed to Fred. Bills, mostly, and a municipal map of Killarney, Ireland. There were also handwritten notes related to Fred's appearance on *The Montel Williams Show*. Under these I found some adult magazines. *Penthouse,* mostly. Inside one magazine I discovered two black-and-white school photographs of teenage girls. The girls' names were visible. The girls were Fred's cousins.

The disordered mess disturbed me. It didn't jibe with the overly controlling image Fred Murray portrayed in public. I didn't see any sense of control here. And the presence of those young girls' photographs inside that adult magazine was troubling.

I left a message on Fred's voice mail, asking him to help me explain some of what I'd seen in Weymouth. But, of course, I never heard back.

THIRTY-TWO

Between the Lines

Outside of the movies, I don't know anybody who talks like Fred Murray. Maura wasn't just abducted, she was "taken by a local dirtbag." Fred wasn't growing old, he was halfway to his "final reward." The police "can't catch a cold" and "the skunk is on their doorstep."

Peter Hyatt is a practitioner of "statement analysis"—finding the hidden subtext behind a person's choice of words. This method of observing a suspect's statement to suss out subconscious intentions harkens to the days of Sherlock Holmes but has come back in vogue thanks to a number of Internet message boards devoted to the idea. Hyatt has offered his insights on high-profile crimes, including the Amanda Knox case. He has written a handbook about statement analysis and offers training through his Web site. While his analysis may never be used as evidence in a court of law, it offers a unique perspective on Fred Murray's choice of language, and a jumping-off point for Hyatt's disciples.

We exchanged messages about Fred's official written statement to police. Here is what Hyatt said:

"Something is very wrong. Note the dropped pronoun 'I' in the first paragraph, and then its appearance later. Note that in 29 lines, he takes 25 to introduce his daughter going missing. The overwhelming number of deceptive statements have lengthy introductions. There is something very bothersome about it. Do police suspect him? Is he just a lousy father, or is there more? They should suspect him.

"It may be that he is deceptive due to purchasing alcohol, driving under the influence, etc., but the focus of that statement is he, himself, and not his missing daughter. At the Quality Inn, he wishes 'not' to be there. Was there anything untoward about their relationship?"

Hyatt posted Fred's statement there so that his readers, his own team of Irregulars, could parse through it.

"Sounds like 3/4 fabrication," one person wrote.

"The 'tale' he tells is so out of order that it makes no sense."

"Why does he call his hotel room 'the' room instead of his room? Is it because he always intended to share it with his daughter?"

"He feels a need to give a reason why he was visiting his daughter. May indicate his intent in going there is questionable (though not necessarily in the context of explaining to the police his reasons for visiting)."

"He justifies why he was there. Akin to alibi building."

Another astute analyst noted something that occurs during Fred's interview on the *Montel* show: Fred slipped into the past tense a few times. When he began to say, "We were buddies," he stopped and switched to "We *are* buddies."

THIRTY-THREE

Petrit Vasi

It's difficult to tell exactly who started the rumor that Maura Murray almost killed Petrit Vasi. Most likely, it began with an anonymous post to one of the message boards devoted to her disappearance: Topix, Websleuths, The Charley Project. Or it might have started on the official Maura Murray Web site run by some of the Murrays' relatives. If that's the case, we'll never know for sure, since the family took their message board down when posters began to speculate about Fred's odd behavior. Whoever started it, the rumor has taken on permanence, because it gives Maura motive to flee.

In 2004, a man named Petrit Vasi was studying economics at UMass. On Thursday, February 5, Vasi and a friend went into town for drinks. Later, Vasi waited outside for a car to pick him up. That's the last thing he remembers.

Police discovered Vasi's limp body on the side of the road at Triangle and Mattoon, near the baseball field, at 12:20 A.M. There were skid marks in the road. It looked like Vasi had been struck by a car, or thrown from a vehicle while riding dangerously. He lay in a coma for several weeks. When he woke up, he told police he had no recollection of what happened to him.

So how does this accident connect to Maura Murray?

February 5 was the night that Maura had her breakdown and cried in front of her supervisor at Melville Hall. Message board commenters suggested that Maura's breakdown was not caused by the phone call from her sister Kathleen; it was caused by her sneaking out to town for a coffee and striking Vasi on the way back. Maybe that's how her Saturn really got damaged, and the accident in New Hampshire was staged to cover up the evidence.

It was a long recovery for Vasi. According to an article in *The Daily Collegian,* it took him six months to walk again.

I tracked down Vasi's sister, Lorina, for an update. Years later, her brother was still not the same person he had been before the accident. The former economics student was working at a car wash in Boston.

"We've stopped looking back on it," she said. "It's hard for everyone. We just look forward now, just thankful we didn't lose him."

It was definitely a hit-and-run, Lorina said.

But from what I learned of Maura's job, it would have been very difficult for her to slip away and return without being noticed and reprimanded for it. There were supervisors touring the campus dorms that night. And Maura's car was not parked nearby.

So why is the Vasi theory still so popular today?

Perhaps it has to do with this message posted to a GeoCities message board:

Maura Murray is NOT a Missing Person
Maura Murray has the right as every independent

adult does to leave with her new boyfriend and start a new life. Maura is living a content and satisfying life in the Province of Quebec.

Maura's father Fred Murray never quite forgave her for being asked to leave West Point. It was his personal bragging point that he had two daughters at West Point. Maura's dismissal damaged Fred's ego and he never completely forgave her.

Maura's being asked to leave West Point and all the ensuing criticism by her father was the beginning of a certain line of thought for Maura, culminating in her leaving on Feb 9, 2004 to start a new life unencumbered by the constant criticism of her father. Maura's relationship with William Rausch was near its end. According to Maura's sister Kathleen, they were having "serious problems." Maura had met someone new, who unlike William Rausch, had no West Point connections and therefore was not a constant reminder to her of her failure at West Point.

On the night of February 5, 2004, Maura took a break from her job at the security desk at a UMass dormitory to go and briefly get coffee and some food.

Sometime between 12 MN and 1 AM Maura driving her Saturn struck and critically injured the UMass student Petrit Vasi leaving him for dead.

Around 1 AM—1:20 AM Feb 6 Maura had a complete emotional breakdown brought on by this hit and run accident. Maura's breakdown was witnessed by a student who reported this to Maura's supervisor, who then came and saw that Maura needed physical help to get back to her dormitory. The supervisor then physically helped Maura back to her dorm and recommended counseling.

Between 2 and 3 AM on the morning of Sunday Feb 8, Maura had a second motor vehicle accident wrecking her father's new car.

Fred Murray's new car was towed around 3 AM to his Hadley motel room. Maura arrived at Fred's motel at the same time as a passenger in the tow truck. Fred was not happy with Maura to put it mildly. What happened in this motel room we'll never know. The next day Maura left for good.

Maura needed to disguise the evidence of the Petrit Vasi hit and run by staging another accident for the purpose of covering up the damage to her car from the Vasi hit and run. She and her new boyfriend travelled in tandem to Route 112 in NH (He was already in Southern NH). The accident was staged, she left her Saturn, walked down the road to where her boyfriend was waiting for her in his car. She disappeared, her only wish is that she be left alone to live her life in peace. She is happy and contented and just wants to be left alone.

In response to this post, a commenter who went by "Observer" wrote:

This is common knowledge in certain circles of people who are close to the family.

And this is where it gets really interesting.

The moderator of the GeoCities forum wanted to find out who "Observer" was. So she contacted a CPA with a background in computers, James Leone, who knew how to trace IP addresses. Leone traced Observer's post to a computer in Taunton, Mass. Then he pored over messages posted on the Topix page devoted to Maura's disappearance, looking for anyone posting from the Taunton area. One avatar stuck out. She posted under the moniker "Citigirl," and claimed to be related to Maura. Were Citigirl and Observer the same person? If so, who was it? Well, hold on to your butts: The Citigirl avatar was linked to a woman named Patti Davidson. Maiden name: Curran. Patricia Curran was one of the young girls in the photographs I had found in that adult magazine at Fred's house in Weymouth.

I called Patricia for comment, but my calls went unreturned.

I started to wonder if it could all be true. Could Maura be laying low in Quebec? Did the family know? Is that why no one was eager for a book to be written?

But then I stumbled upon some information about a series of murders that occurred not far from where Maura disappeared that made me question my theory of the tandem driver. Was it possible that a prolific New England serial killer, who had gone dormant for a decade, had returned?

THIRTY-FOUR

The Shadow of Death Returns

It's possible the killings started as early as 1968 with the murder of Joanne Dunham, but nobody can say for sure. It was the beginning of summer, the end of classes. The pretty-as-pie fifteen-year-old was last seen walking away from the Raiche mobile home park in Charlestown, New Hampshire, heading for the bus stop. Her body was found the next afternoon on a roped-off dirt road in nearby Unity. She had been raped and asphyxiated.

The unsolved murders along the Connecticut River Valley began in earnest in 1978. On October 24, twenty-seven-year-old Cathy Millican visited the Chandler Brook Wetland Preserve in New London, to photograph birds. Someone stabbed her twenty-nine times and tossed her body into the marsh. In 1981, a thirty-seven-year-old woman named Mary Elizabeth Critchley was last seen hitchhiking near the Vermont/Mass border on Route 91. By the time her body was found, it was so decomposed that no one could determine the cause of death. There was also Bernice

Courtemanche, a friendly sixteen-year-old nurse's aide, last seen in Claremont on May 30, 1984. Her skeleton was found two years later off Cat Hole Road, in Newport. Four more followed: Ellen Fried, Eva Morse, Lynda Moore, and Barbara Agnew.

The abductions and "dump sites" were concentrated along a short stretch of Route 91 between the Mass border and White River Junction. Investigators attempted to find some connection between the women. All were white. Some worked for the local phone company. Courtemanche, Fried, and Agnew worked in area hospitals. Detectives wondered if their serial killer could be a tow truck driver, cruising rest stops and lonely roads. One woman's body was found in deep snow, and only a very large truck or Jeep could have gotten to the site.

In 1988, the Connecticut River Valley Killer was nearly caught. Twenty-two-year-old Jane Boroski stopped at a convenience store in West Swanzey on her way home from the county fair. This was in the southwest corner of New Hampshire, a town with a covered bridge. Boroski was seven months pregnant, but that didn't stop the man in the Jeep Wagoneer. When she returned to her car, he stabbed her twenty-seven times and left her for dead.

Boroski was a tough woman, though. With two collapsed lungs, a severed jugular, and a bleeding kidney, she drove to a friend's house. She lived. So did her daughter, though the child suffered from mild cerebral palsy because of the attack.

A police sketch artist sat down with Boroski and got a good rendering of her attacker. Height: about 5 feet 8 inches. Maybe 160 pounds. Between thirty and forty years old, with sandy-blond hair and a high forehead. Detectives sent the composite sketch to the papers. And then the serial killer stopped killing. It's possible he committed suicide or was sent to prison for another crime or simply moved away. Or the Boroski incident might have scared him so much he took a break. It wouldn't have been without precedent.

Dennis Rader, the so-called BTK Killer—as in "bind-torture-kill"—took breaks from killing, too. The Wichita dog-catcher stopped murdering in 1991 and wasn't caught until 2004. He quit preying on women because he was raising a family and his sadistic hobby was too time-consuming. He was about to begin again, he says, when police finally caught up with him.

Could the Connecticut River Valley Killer have resurfaced? Was he responsible for the abductions of Brianna Maitland and Maura Murray? Both women vanished just north of the predator's old killing fields.

An excellent book on the Connecticut River Valley murders was published in 1993. Written by journalist Philip E. Ginsburg, *The Shadow of Death* is an intimate account of the search for one of America's most prolific serial killers. Ginsburg's primary source was one of the first independent criminal profilers, a gonzo psychologist named John Philpin, author of seven true crime books of his own and a frequent commenter on news programs when a girl goes missing.

I looked at Philpin's press photo, and I saw my future. Worry lines concealed behind a grizzled beard; eyes that had peered beyond the pale. He'd be the first to admit the work weighs on him. I tracked him down one day and was not surprised to learn that he'd already consulted on the Maura Murray investigation.

Philpin does not believe that the Connecticut River Valley Killer has resurfaced. He believes he knows who is responsible for those crimes: a tow truck driver who committed suicide a while back. He thinks the key to finding out what happened to Maura is to learn more about her past. But it's hard to really get an understanding of Maura's past when you have to deal with Fred Murray.

"The dad has info he isn't sharing," Philpin said. "I never believed Fred. Not one word. There was something very wrong about that man. He created so many smoke screens nobody could get a handle on him. Fred wanted total control of Maura's life. And there was an unnatural and unusual closeness between father and daughter."

THIRTY-FIVE

Motive

Casey was expelled from preschool shortly after his Christmas program, for behavior that included hitting, biting, scratching, and running away. The coup de grace was when he walked up to the young woman who assisted his teacher and slapped her ass like he was Boss Hogg at the Boar's Nest.

I asked him later, "Why did you do that?"

"She wasn't being nice to me," he said. "So I spanked her."

I know what you're thinking: It was learned behavior. It must all be learned behavior, right? The hitting, the running away . . . What must be going on behind closed doors? Yes, I did spank him. We tried everything, remember? Time-outs. Positive reinforcement. Diversion. And spanking. A quick swat on his tokus. He'd been spanked maybe five times in his life. We stopped because whenever we spanked Casey he became so offended by our actions that he grew even more belligerent. I was beginning to understand that, on some level, Casey considered himself our equal. Who were we to punish *him*?

I explained to my son how lucky he was that we didn't spank him anymore. I told him how, when I was his age, my dad used to come at me with a belt or ask me to go get a thin branch from a tree out back. How my dad's dad used to just fucking punch him until he quit whining. But the story didn't slow Casey down any and the next time we visited my dad, he asked him about the belt because he wanted to see it.

"I think pain is funny," he said one day, out of the blue.

We started seeing a counselor, a woman younger than my wife. Casey played with LEGOS while we talked about him. Hard to tell if any of it was getting through.

Julie found a new Montessori in Akron. The kind Indian woman who ran the place spoke to us in a gentle tone and assured us that no one in the history of her Montessori had ever been turned away based on behavior and Casey would not be the first. He lasted five weeks. When I came to pick him up that last day, I reminded her of what she had said to me when we met. She wasn't kicking my son out, she explained. Her school just wasn't the place Casey should be anymore.

Around this time I started smoking weed again.

My buddy Ben was having a rough time. He was a sitting juror on a capital murder case, the kind that was on the news every night. He was thinking about sending the defendant to prison for the rest of his life. And yet he was in awe of the defense attorney's skill in the courtroom. "You ever get in trouble," he told me, "you get that Roger Synenberg. Don't forget that name. Roger Synenberg."

Ben was from a town in Pennsylvania called Kecksburg, famous for the UFO that supposedly crashed there in 1965. A friend of his grew wonderful marijuana in the woods near the crash site. Couple times a year, Ben went home and brought back some of that Kecksburg Express. The first time I tried it, I didn't feel a thing until Ben suddenly shrank before my eyes to the size of a midget. Kecksburg weed will fuck up a seasoned pot smoker. And oh the times we had.

It smelled like my childhood. Like going home. It helped me relax after spending the day hunting serial killers and missing women.

I got some interesting news around this time.

"I think there's a second pink line here," said Julie. She handed me the plastic wand. At first I didn't see it. Then I did. It was faint. Very faint. But, yeah. There it was.

We had been trying for months, but I had started to think it might not be possible on the Cymbalta. The doctor confirmed it. Julie was pregnant.

I didn't know what I was more afraid of: that it would be another boy, or that it would be a girl brought into a world full of dangerous men.

In January of 2012, I found a better motive for Maura to disappear—better than fleeing after the Vasi hit-and-run.

I was blanketing the police departments in the areas near where Maura had lived with generic public records requests. In the newsroom, we called this "going fishing." Sometimes it kicked up a new lead for an article, usually it was a waste of time. Low risk. High reward. I got lucky. A public records request to the Amherst Police Department found a larceny report. Credit card fraud. At the time of her disappearance, Maura was in a lot of trouble with the law.

On November 3, 2003, a UMass student contacted Amherst

police. She'd checked her bank account online and had noticed charges to restaurants that she'd never been to: La Cucina di Pinocchio, Domino's, and Papa Gino's in nearby Hadley. Someone had racked up debt on her credit card, purchasing about $80 worth of pizza.

Police phoned the restaurants and asked the managers to review receipts for the nights in question. The pizzas, it turned out, were all delivered to Kennedy Hall.

Later that same night, the manager at Pinocchio's phoned Officer Carlos Rivera at the Amherst police station. A woman had just called and ordered a pizza using the stolen credit card number. Rivera told the manager to make the delivery.

Rivera and another officer, David Pinkham, drove out to Kennedy Hall and waited. The pizza guy arrived. A young woman signed for the food. As soon as she handed the receipt to the driver, the policemen swooped in. It was Maura Murray.

When they walked her back to her room, Pinkham told her to come clean. Maura said she got the credit card numbers off a Pinocchio's receipt she'd found on the ground. When Rivera pointed out that receipts from Pinocchio's did not include full credit card numbers, she said she must have gotten it off a receipt from a different pizza place.

Pinkham asked Maura how she remembered the number. But Maura only looked at the ground. He told her to get whatever paper she kept the number on and give it to him. She fished through a drawer and came back with a note card that had the credit card number on it. There were other numbers on the card, too. Several. Maura told him they were her friends' phone numbers.

Again, Pinkham asked her why she did it. But Maura wouldn't answer. He took her picture and informed her that they would need her to come in to the station soon to make a statement.

On November 9, Maura sat down with Officer Rivera. From his report: "[Maura] acknowledged she had used the credit card illegally, but did not give a reason why. It is unknown how exactly the credit card number was retrieved...."

Rivera told Maura that she would be charged with unauthorized use of a credit card, a misdemeanor that carried the possibility of a $500 fine and up to a year in jail. On December 16, Maura went to court and was found guilty. Luckily, the judge ordered that the charge be dismissed under the condition that Maura stay out of trouble for six months. Maura's record would have been wiped clean in June 2004.

But...

But after a night of drinking, Maura crashed her father's car into a guardrail while driving to his hotel room at three in the morning. She wasn't charged with drunken driving, but a reckless op charge was in the works, according to the officer who responded to the scene. Maura was going to be cited for the accident, but she disappeared first. Did Maura think that the larceny charge would come back now that she'd gotten in trouble again?

Maura was studying to be a nurse. What hospital would hire her with a fraud charge on her record?

She kept her court appearances secret from friends and family. Billy never knew.

Here's what we do know: The day before she disappeared, Maura gave her nursing scrubs to a classmate. She packed up her room. And by Monday evening, Maura was gone for good.

"It's a girl," the technician said, pointing to three black marks on a monitor. The black marks represented a vagina, I guess. Julie squeezed my hand and smiled, then clapped her hands and shouted, "Yay!"

"You sure?" I asked.

"Yes."

The possible sum of my daughter's life swept past my mind's eye—all the intersections of trouble, the random acts of violence we never see coming, the decades of risk that awaited her. And I was responsible for her. There's a fine line between delusion and vision, between paranoia and risk management. I'm constantly telling myself that just because I have a daughter doesn't mean she'll end up like Maura Murray. And it started that day.

"Well, all right," I said. "All right."

My wife wanted to name her Amy. But we couldn't, because I'd written a book about a girl named Amy who'd been abducted and murdered. So we thought on it.

What will she look like? I wondered. What will my girl look like? And what will I do to protect her for the rest of her life? As a father, what wouldn't I do to keep her out of trouble?

THIRTY-SIX

112dirtbag

On February 8, 2012, the eighth anniversary of Maura's disappearance, I got a call from one of my Irregulars as I was watching TV with my family. The man's name was Lance Reenstierna, a videographer from Boston who has his own company called Lucky Quarter Productions. "You gotta see this clip that just went up on YouTube," he said.

Lance had a Google alert set for any new posts related to Maura Murray. Apparently, someone had used Maura's name in the metadata of a short video that had been uploaded to YouTube that day from an account named "112dirtbag." I pulled it up. The video is silent. It's a single image on slow zoom: a pink ski lift ticket for Bretton Woods Mountain Resort, dated February 11, 2004. The Bretton slopes are north of Haverhill a bit, over by Mount Washington. The ticket is part of an "adult lodging package" purchased two days after Maura's accident.

"What do you think?" he asked.

"I'm not sure," I said. Was someone suggesting that Maura had gone skiing? Was this some kind of evidence?

Lance called me again, a few minutes later. His voice was different this time. He sounded frightened. "A new video just went up from the same account," he said.

I watched it while Lance stayed on the phone with me.

Slow dissolve into the face of an older man peering into the camera. His head is bald on top, the hair cropped short and gray on the sides. Large ears. He wears glasses and the lenses reflect the blue square of a computer screen. The man appears to be missing several teeth. Behind him is a concrete wall, barely lit. He is laughing. A chuckle that becomes a cackle. And then he stops. And smiles. A piano plays a melancholy tune in the background, Chopin's Waltz No. 3 (op. 34 no. 2). Fade to black. Words appear on-screen: *Happy Anniversary.*

"What the hell?" I said.

"Who is that man?"

"I have no idea."

I felt goose bumps break out over my skin. The hair on the back of my neck bristled. I could feel my heart beating in my chest. Was a killer reaching out over YouTube to taunt investigators on the anniversary of Maura's disappearance? I decided to not say anything to Julie until I had more information. Every time I drive into the White Mountains, I have to assure her that I'm never in any real danger. I sent the link to law enforcement. Then I embedded the video on my blog. Who was this man? I asked. Did anyone know?

A short time later, 112dirtbag removed both videos and deleted his account. Luckily, Lance had already grabbed copies. I uploaded the two videos to my YouTube account and reposted. Whoever 112dirtbag was, he was having second thoughts about his confession, if that's what this was. He must have gotten spooked when he saw the view count climbing and tried to go to ground. My Irregulars now had a common target. Soon, they were working together to uncover the identity of 112dirtbag. Someone posted the link on Reddit and a stream of people who had never heard of Maura Murray were suddenly poring over my blog.

One reader noted that the reflection in 112dirtbag's glasses seemed to show my blog.

Somewhere along the line, people began to threaten the man, whoever he was. A lynch-mob mentality percolated in the comments.

One clever reader noticed similarities between 112dirtbag and the profile of a man who had posted on a Topix message board devoted to Maura's disappearance. He was known as "Beagle" on Topix, and he sometimes wrote rambling posts blaming UMass researchers for Maura's abduction, claiming they had harvested her eggs for scientific experiments.

Here's an excerpt from one of Beagle's posts:

> "What do antioxidants (aka vitamins, nutritional supplements) do? They fight off free radicals. What do free radicals do? They reduce the length of the chromosomes telomeres.
>
> Molly Bish, Maura Murray, and Lindsay Ferguson were attacked because they were, biologically, highly desirable organisms."

Beagle's profile photo resembled the scary laughing man who posted on YouTube as 112dirtbag. But it was hard to tell for sure, because the laughing man was cast in shadow in some dirty basement. I couldn't help but wonder: Was he keeping women in that basement?

Then someone dug up a personal blog that Beagle had used as a diary, writing vignettes about his time spent homeless in Massachusetts, living out of his van and working as a Wal-Mart greeter near UMass.

On February 10, a new video was uploaded to YouTube, this time through the account "Mr112Dirtbag." The most cryptic message so far, it was a computer-generated painting of a bald man's head next to some symbolic code. Four numbers and a red zigzag. 1, 5, 27, 8. Was it a map to Maura's body? What was Mr112Dirtbag trying to tell us?

One commenter noted that Mr112Dirtbag alluded to another cold case in the metadata of this newest post, which referenced a news article about the unsolved murder of Daniel Croteau, a thirteen-year-old boy whose body was found lying facedown in the Chicopee River on April 15, 1972. Chicopee is a short drive from Amherst. Was it 1, 5 for "15"? Did he reverse 72 to make 27? Was he claiming responsibility for this crime, too? Police had a good suspect for Croteau's murder, a defrocked priest. Did they have the wrong man?

The Croteau connection took us to yet another post by Beagle, on the Bismark, North Dakota Topix board, where he admitted to being questioned as a suspect in the Maura Murray case:

> The MA PI [private investigator] would not have wasted his time asking me whether or not I killed Maura if he thought the answer could not have been yes. Most likely he looked at the totality of my answer. Although I vocalized a strongly confident no (because I didn't kill her), I'm not sure how he might have read the rest of my answer—that is, my body language. See the old Reid Interrogation Technique for a better answer. I'm

also told there is a video game called LA Noir, in which the character(s) use some kind of software to evaluate whether or not subjects are telling the truth.

"It's also true that LE [law enforcement], such as Mass. State Police, will use experts to help them investigate a difficult case. This particular MA PI would be an easy fit because of his previous experience as a detective in MSP and former head of its Behavioral Sciences Unit. He's very good at his job and has contracted to gov't. before.

Or maybe it has something to do with [John] Stobierski's civil suit against the Springfield MA Roman Catholic Diocese. Stobierski, a Greenfield MA attorney in private practice, represents the family of murdered thirteen-year-old altar boy Daniel Croteau. When I showed Stobierski, who had worked on the Molly Bish [homicide] a phone bill I found relating to the Bish case, he became instantly upset and told me to get this junk (copy of the phone bill) off his desk.

It was apparent to me that Mr112Dirtbag was now posting more videos in response to the attention he was getting from my blog. I was feeding this man's obsessions, making him a celebrity. We were having a conversation, the journalist and the maniac. And though I did not know who he was, he was very aware of me.

Before he set his sights on my son, Beagle posted one more video that linked him to a horrific killing spree in New Hampshire and a brazen escape from a mental ward for the criminally insane.

THIRTY-SEVEN

Mr. 1974

Beagle/112dirtbag/Mr112Dirtbag never left his videos up for long. But Lance Reenstierna downloaded them before they could be removed. Lance was on constant alert and sometimes only had five minutes to grab the new clip. On Valentine's Day, Beagle posted three new videos.

In a clip titled "No Hope for Mental Wannabe," Beagle wears a Panama hat and plays an electric keyboard in a dingy basement. The basement is furnished. There are old wood-paneled walls and steps leading to the ground floor. He dances like a character out of a David Lynch movie and the whole thing ends with a shot of him playing the sax.

Clip number two, titled "Bodies of Water," is a video of a stone bridge shot from inside a car during a summer rainstorm. Superimposed titles and soft music make this clip seem like the opening of a horror film. It reads: *Sassamon Films presents Colleen Reston; Kenneth Patton; Directed by Tracy Adamson.*

In the third clip, Beagle is dressed like a member of a road construction crew: yellow reflective vest, hard hat. This one is titled: "Man Loses It." He looks at the camera and says, in a manufactured southern drawl, "Hi, I'm Mr. 1974." He goes silent for twenty seconds, then says, "I'm not Mr. 1974. I'm a private detective, isn't that right, Dr. Anthony?" Then he plays with a jar of pink slime, getting his fingers sticky and wet. "Happy New Year," he says at the end. "And drive safe."

The Irregulars went right to work, trying to uncover the hidden clues behind the Valentine's Day posts. The best anyone could do on "Sassamon" was that it might refer to a golf course called Sassamon Trace, in Natick, Mass. Or it could be an obscure reference to John Sassamon, a Native American interpreter, born about 1600, whose assassination started King Philip's War. The other names were not real actors. But I have a theory. I think they might all be doctors. Kenneth Patton and Tracy Adamson are the names of doctors in Cincinnati. And there's a psychiatrist named Dr. Colleen Blanchfield who works in Reston, Virginia. Had Beagle once been a patient?

But "Mr. 1974"? What the hell did that mean? What happened in 1974 that was important to this man?

An Irregular named Mike was the first to make the connection to one of New Hampshire's most frightening unsolved mysteries. John William McGrath was seventeen years old when he took the rifle his uncle had reclaimed from a dead Japanese soldier in WWII and used it to shoot his two younger brothers to death. McGrath waited for his parents to get home, then killed them, too. This all happened in Newport, New Hampshire, in 1962.

According to articles published in *The Boston Globe* and the *Concord Monitor,* McGrath was a star student at Towle High School, voted "class intellectual" by his classmates. He had applied to Dartmouth, and was preparing to play the lead in the school play, *The Male Animal*. But in a single night, he murdered his entire family. Then he drove forty-five minutes to a Concord mental hospital and calmly turned himself in to the night nurse.

In 1965, a grand jury refused to press charges against McGrath for the murders because he was insane (it was a different time, folks). McGrath was the ideal patient inside the walls of the mental hospital he was committed to. He wrote book reviews. He painted murals of covered bridges on the hospital walls. By 1969, he'd progressed so much that the superintendent, Dr. Warren Burns, recommended him for conditional parole. McGrath was allowed to take computer classes at New Hampshire Tech, under supervision, of course.

The new freedom proved too much of a temptation, though. McGrath started bringing drugs into the hospital. Then he burglarized the pharmacy. The new super sent him to prison. He returned to the hospital in 1972. Then, in 1974, he simply walked away from the hospital grounds. He has been missing ever since.

As Lieutenant Barry Hunter of the Sullivan County Sheriff's Department likes to tell reporters: "He could be in a pauper's grave in Cleveland, Ohio, or a popular businessman in California, or anywhere in between."

I thought McGrath's black-and-white mug shot looked familiar when I pulled it up on my computer. McGrath had a receding forehead, even at seventeen, thin brown hair on the sides. He wore glasses and his ears were overlarge—like Beagle's. Like Beagle, McGrath wrote intelligent prose, was adept at computers, and had a knack for painting. Could it be?

By the end of February, Beagle's videos were international news. Nothing makes an unsolved mystery more thrilling than a psychotic man posting clues about the case on the Internet.

Britain's *Daily Mail* ran a story. Boston's Fox affiliate interviewed John Healy, who said, "This has no credibility to me at all." The Murray family released a statement: "The family is deeply saddened to learn and view that a seemingly clinically disturbed individual would post misleading and cruel videos online. The family respectfully requests the public to ignore and disregard this hideous information and allow investigators to pursue leads of substance and credibility."

When I finally told my wife about Beagle, she asked me if there was anything to be worried about—if he might want to harm me, show up at our house with a gun or something. I reminded Julie what my first editor, Pete Kotz, told me when I was researching the Amy Mihaljevic murder for *Scene*. "You got nothing to fuckin' worry about. Nobody ever goes after the journalist," he said. "If they get mad at what you wrote, they'll go after your source. But you? You're fine."

THIRTY-EIGHT

Family

On May 6, Beagle posted a new video. I clicked the link when it arrived in my in-box. As it began to play, I felt my blood run cold. A variety of emotions washed over me. First it was fear. But that quickly dissolved into anger, which condensed into a nugget of pure rage.

It was a video of my five-year-old son. It looked like footage from a camera, taken of Casey from a parked car near our home. But then I realized it was actually a collection of still photographs. I had taken these pictures. They were family photos I had posted on my private Facebook timeline. Casey playing in front of our house. Casey smiling for the camera.

Julie sat beside me on the couch. Casey was asleep upstairs.

Who do I call? The police? Which police? Akron? Amherst? Haverhill, New Hampshire? *Fuck*. Who do I call about this?

As I was thinking it through, the video was deleted. He must have been watching the view count, knowing I had the alerts set up and I would be one of the first to see it. Once the video reached its audience—me—he took it down. Too fast for my friends in Boston to grab it from YouTube. Now, there was no evidence.

Another video came up in its place. This one was just a black screen with a single word: RENNER.

He was teasing me.

The Cymbalta keeps me calm. I'm a calm guy. I am. But there's a freedom in blind rage once you give yourself over to it that is as welcoming as any drug. On the other side of rage is a certain calm. The eye of the hurricane. I found that place, at age eight, when I was beaten by my stepmother. Her beatings taught me where to find it. I had forgotten how good it felt to give myself over to that pure hatred, that realm of vengeance where you don't care about consequence or morality. *Beat me. Beat me. See if I care. You're not getting tears from me. Not today. Today all you get is this smile.* I didn't want to call the cops, I realized. I wanted Beagle for myself. Because I knew him for what he was: a crazy man only pretending to be dangerous. And he had no idea who I really was: a dangerous man working really hard not to be crazy. If I had known, truly known, who Beagle was that night, I would have driven a thousand miles to his doorstep.

Instead, I got drunk. Good and drunk. Beer. Then whiskey until I forgot myself and my anger. And when I woke, hungover, I cuddled with Casey on the couch and watched *SpongeBob* and took more Cymbalta and thought about other things.

Later that week, I contacted the New Hampshire State Police and the prosecutor's office, but nobody was interested in filing charges against an online avatar.

"Dad?" Casey asked me one day, in as serious a voice as the kid can muster.

"Yeah, what's up?"

"When will you die?"

I wondered if he had heard some of the conversations I'd had that day, about Beagle. Could he sense there was some danger? "Not for a long time," I said. "Not until you have kids and they have kids of their own."

"Okay," he said. "But when you die, can I have your iPhone?"

"Push, babe," I said. "Push, sweetie."

It was August 4. We were at Akron City, not the hospital we had planned to be at for this delivery. Akron General turned us away. No room at the inn. Julie's amniotic fluid was running low and, just to be on the safe side, she wanted an induction. It was early evening when she arrived. A baby girl slipped into the world and suddenly we had two children, one of each.

We named her Laine. Julie calls her Lainey. I call her Laineybug, or Lois Laine.

"I think she has red hair," the nurse said. "Does it run in the family?"

I cringed. "My grandfather," I said.

While we were resting that night, a nurse came in and told us about the man who'd walked into Akron General and shot his wife to death. It happened the same time Lainey was born. If we had been there, as planned, I might have passed the guy in the hall, on the way to tell our parents the good news. What would have happened in that alternate universe? How much of life is coincidence? How much is fate?

In September, a police sergeant sent me an e-mail.

"I had a recent Town of Chatham resident of ours call me concerned about information he learned about his brother," she wrote. "Alden Olson is a man known to us for his past odd behavior towards his family as well as disturbing Internet postings. He has been involved with YouTube postings for the 'Happy Anniversary' of Maura's disappearance. This came to our attention when our resident (who has an active restraining order against the man) called me to show me the blog posts he found dated Feb 21, 2012, related to Maura. The man in this and probably the deleted related videos is Alden Olson, last known address of Hadley, MA though we have dealt with him previously in Greenfield, MA back in 2007. He was then known to go under the sign-on name 'Storagehead' and family have identified him on this video under 'mr112dirtbag.' He has been known to voice his theories and opinions online in a very eccentric manner. Please contact me for anything further on this."

I knew who 112dirtbag was now.

But I let him go.

He was just another crank, and I had other things to worry about. Night feedings. Diapers. Better things. Fuck him, too.

THIRTY-NINE

Bad Rabbit

I was frustrated by the lack of cooperation from Maura's family. A case like this can't be successfully investigated without access to primary sources. So I decided to try Billy's mom, Sharon Rausch, again, since she lived closest to me.

Sharon was not home, so I canvassed the neighbors, hoping to get lucky and find someone who'd met Maura during her stays in Ohio. Across the street was a guy named Rick who ran an auto shop out of his garage. Billy's dad's truck was in there. Rick was fixing it for the Rausch family before they left on vacation.

"We grew up here, Billy's dad and I," said Rick, a burly, friendly man. "I moved away, then come back. It's a different world now. We all lost so much." He pointed down the road. "Neighbors over there lost two kids in an accident. Then, Maura. And a'course Billy's sister. I come home one night, see all the cop cars. She shot herself in the basement."

* * *

Morrow County is one of those sparse regions of central Ohio where the roads go on for endless stretches between fields of corn. There's not much need for a coroner to tally up the dead. The part-time Morrow County coroner was a doctor named William Lee, who had a private practice in Cardington, inside a squat ranch home beside Gary's Discount Outlet. Dr. Lee was a short Asian fellow with a severe accent and a soft voice. I had to ask him to repeat everything so I could make sure I heard him correctly.

"Heather Rausch had history of depression," he explained. "Attempts at suicide. It was very sad. And I never found out what she wanted with the sheriff."

"Excuse me?" I said. "What about the sheriff?"

"The day she killed herself, she was trying to talk to the sheriff. Said she knew something about some illegal activity. Wanted to talk. I never found out what that was all about."

I had found a rabbit hole.

During any missing-persons investigation, one encounters a number of rabbit holes: avenues of inquiry that open up under your feet, leading you on a ride toward some answer. Only one of those rabbit holes will lead to the solution, though. The others, no matter how good they seem at first, dead-end in happenstance or coincidence. I remember in the Amy Mihaljevic case, I came across this suspect who worked at the local zoo. I found out that he crossed paths with Amy shortly before her murder. When I checked his work records I saw that he'd called in sick the day she was abducted. I questioned him about it, and discovered he was friends with another missing girl, Amanda Berry. Had to be him, right? It wasn't. As likely as he seemed, he just wasn't the guy. I lost myself in that rabbit hole for a while.

So, this Heather Rausch thing. Was it a good lead or a weird dead end? I mean, the first place your mind goes when you hear that Heather needed to talk to the sheriff is that she must have some information about Maura Murray, right? Or at least that's where I was. That's what I was thinking.

I got the police report on Heather's suicide. A police officer was dispatched to the Rausch residence at 5:39 A.M. the morning of April 20, 2007. From his narrative on the death of Heather Rausch, aged thirty-four:

"When I entered the home, I noticed an older female standing in the kitchen area and she directed me to a bedroom on the west end of the house. As I entered the bedroom, I noticed that there was a blond haired female laying on the floor in a large pool of blood. . . . I immediately checked for a pulse but could not find one. . . . I looked at the bedroom door and noticed a small hole and could see that the door had been kicked in. I looked around the room and could see a small caliber revolver lying on the floor about 12 inches just west of the victim."

Bill (Billy's father) and Sharon Rausch told the officer that they had gone to bed around 5 A.M. and then were awakened by a loud "crack." Heather, they said, had spoken of suicide and so Bill had hidden his gun from her. After the crack, he went to find it. It was still there. But it turned out she had purchased another one, in Indiana, a Smith & Wesson .38. That's the one they found by her body.

"Chief Deputy Davis and Dr. Lee entered [the] crime scene. EMT Wolfe was able to locate a white piece of paper in the victim's waistband. He gave the paper to Deputy Brane and I collected it as evidence. The paper was a note the victim had left on her person."

I looked through the remainder of the report. The note wasn't there.

"Where's the suicide note?" I asked the records officer.

"You can't have it," she said.

"Why?"

"The case is still open. Detectives are still investigating it for possible criminal charges."

Well. Now I was intrigued. I had never come across a suicide that was treated as an open and active investigation. There were, I knew, two possible explanations for this. One: The detectives suspected there was another crime connected to Heather Rausch's suicide. Two: They were keeping the suicide "open" as a way to keep the suicide note private. In the State of Ohio, many police files can remain secret until a case is officially closed or a suspect is indicted.

I pushed back as hard as I could. I mailed a new round of official public records requests to Charles Howland, the Morrow County prosecutor. Howland, I learned, had a reputation for disrespecting the First Amendment. A staunch old-school Republican, he never made things easy for the media. For instance, he would not make copies of 911 tapes, insisting reporters listen to the calls and take notes instead. I asked him for a document called a Vaughn Index on the redacted material, which might have forced him to officially explain why he was withholding the records.

In the end, Howland must have figured it would just be easier to let me see the damn thing. They provided me with a copy of Heather's handwritten note. It is a very private document and I will not go into detail. Suffice it to say, there is no connection to Maura Murray. Maura is never mentioned in the note. Most of it centers on Heather's problems getting proper psychiatric help and instructions about what to do with her remains.

But what of Dr. Lee's insistence that Heather had something important to tell the sheriff? I put that question to Sheriff Steven Brenneman. But he said he and his detectives had never heard from her.

Heather Rausch's suicide was a curious distraction, but I am convinced it's a dead end. One of those bad rabbit holes. Some families are magnets for tragedy. It's been my experience that those who have suffered the most are usually the first ones to suffer again. Luck. Sometimes it's shitty and that's the way it is. I cross myself every day, asking for happiness. I never take it for granted, because my family knows about tragedy, too.

FORTY

An Overdue Visit

Here's my favorite part about what I do. There comes a time in every true crime story where the reporter goes to the bad guy's house to ask him tough questions. Did you rape this woman? Did you kill this girl? Sometimes, that reporter is the only person who will ever ask those questions, because the police don't have enough evidence to bring him in. I've traveled to poor, flophouse burbs outside Steubenville to locate a serial killer's nephew so that I could ask him if he'd helped with some of the killings. I've been chased out of a used car lot by a man who probably murdered three people. I flew to Key West to confront a man I thought might have taken Amy Mihaljevic.

I'm not sure why I enjoy these moments. Oftentimes I make these house calls late at night, when no one would be able to see them pull me into their basements. It would be safer during the day, so why do I go at night? It's the danger, right? I enjoy the look on their face when I ask the question, that moment when the mask breaks in the shock of the confrontation and I get a glimpse of the monster on the other side, the beast that only their victims have ever seen. Some believe these killers are psychological abnormalities. Others believe these people are possessed by demons. Whatever. There's something very powerful about looking a monster in the eyes and showing it that you're not afraid.

One day in the first week of January 2013, I drove into Alliance, Ohio, to knock on a monster's door. He lived on North Union in this empty steel-mill town, in a tall house surrounded by a tall fence. I knocked on the door and after a few moments, he ambled onto his porch. His mask was nice enough: a pleasant, elderly man's face; a high widow's peak; his red hair gone gray; a paunch under his short-sleeve button-up, between brown suspenders.

"Do you remember me?" I asked.

He crinkled his eyes and smiled but shook his head. "I should. I know that. I do know you. But I can't place it."

"I'm James Renner," I said. "Last time you saw me, I was a kid. I grew up and now I'm a writer. I came by to let you know that I'm writing about you on Monday."

"You're Jimmy," he said, eyes wide now.

I nodded. "I'm your grandson."

My uncle Michael contacted me at the end of 2012. I hadn't seen him in twenty-four years. He found me on Facebook and invited me out for pizza. We met at Luigi's, in Akron. The dining room was full. He was finally ready to talk about his father and he needed a writer to tell the story. Until that day, I'd heard only snippets of the tale, from my mother, but enough to know my grandfather was a dangerous man.

For many years, my mom thought her father was dead. Before

she was old enough to have many memories of him, he disappeared. She was told that her father had died in a car crash on Seven-Hill Road coming back from the bar. My mother and her three sisters went to live with family on a farm in Charlestown. Then, around 1975, my mom discovered that her old man was alive. He'd actually started a new family in Alliance.

My aunt—let's call her Peg—was twelve when she left the farm to stay with my grandfather, Keith Simpkins, in Alliance. He gave Peg her own room and a new bike. She felt like a girl who finds out she's an orphaned princess. Keith was damn near perfect. Active in the church. A leader in the local Boy Scout troop. A mentor at A.A. Soon, Keith was raping her every day.

He'd ply her with booze and pot and then tie her to the bed and gag her so that she wouldn't make a sound. Sometimes it happened after school, but most times it was at night when everyone else was in bed. He'd whistle to himself on the way to her room.

On Saturdays, he took Peg to Acme Hard Chrome (now Acme Industrial Group, on Freedom Avenue), where he plated metal. He'd rape her in his office. Once, when Peg hosted a birthday party, Keith went after one of her friends. The girl called her parents to pick her up. No charges were filed.

"I turned him in to the counselor at Stanton Middle," my aunt recalled. "I showed them the bruises all up and down my thighs. They called him and brought him into the room with me and he denied it. Said I was just a hood kid trying to cause trouble."

Peg's oldest sister—call her Anne—made a pact with Keith: She wouldn't resist when he raped her so long as he never went after her younger sisters. She didn't find out until later that he'd lied to her.

Couple years later, Keith started raping another daughter, "Susan," too.

As a kid, I never knew any of this. My mother suspected, but she had no firsthand knowledge—although there was one time when Keith got drunk and told my mother in a low voice how much she looked like my grandma when they were kids. I spent a lot of time at his house on North Union with my little sister. Holidays, mostly. Sundays for football. His kitchen always smelled like sloppy joes and coffee. We were never left alone with him. I still see the layout of his house in my dreams: the framed painting of the praying man in the living room, the *Saturday Evening Post* in the bathroom upstairs.

He had a dog that could talk. He did. It said, "Momma," and "I love you." Sometimes he would invite the older kids to watch marathons of Rocky movies in the basement where the dog slept. I couldn't wait for the day when he would invite me down there.

We were pen pals for a bit. My grandpa was a storyteller. He'd write me long stories, most of them funny, on tall sheets of yellow legal paper, the sort of paper lawyers and reporters use.

Then one day in 1989, around the time Amy Mihaljevic vanished, my mother told me, simply, that my grandfather was a very evil man and that we would never see him again. Her sisters—my aunts—had finally told each other about the rapes. Some had found the strength to speak out after years of therapy, of A.A. And now their own children were old enough to catch Keith's eye and there were far too many of us to keep safe. They couldn't keep it quiet anymore.

This revelation changed each of us in different ways. Most of us just had this weird empty spot in our family tree that was hard to explain to curious friends. Odd, but nothing tragic. My aunts, though, had to explain to their husbands why they were cutting off contact with their father. That meant taking a good hard look at how fucked up their lives were because of this one man. And they were less able to handle this because of their own alcoholism, drug abuse, and physical deteriorations, all precipitated by Keith's years of abusing them.

This revelation caused divorces. Mental breakdowns. A nuclear bomb went off, irradiating fucking *everything*. And the worst part was that Keith remained unharmed, clean, a respected member of society. He even had the audacity to get sober.

It directly affected me, too, beginning at age five, when my parents divorced. Years later, my mother would confess that she'd never fought for custody because she was afraid all of this would come out in court.

And in the quiet, my grandfather never stopped his predations.

My uncle Michael lived with Keith back then. He was about fourteen and I was seven when I was still going over there regularly. Michael had a STOP sign on his bedroom door that I thought was pretty badass (though now I realize, literally as I'm writing this, how that sign was a not-so-subtle plea to his father). Michael taught me how to play Othello. I thought he was the coolest.

It was difficult to listen to the stories he told me at Luigi's that afternoon.

"His thing was to perform masturbation rituals on me—orally stimulate my penis to force me to have an erection; that's how he would get me to have anal sex with him," Michael explained. "His favorite location was in the basement of our house. There was a putrid blanket covered with dog fur he kept in front of the door—that was our dog Rebel's bed. He would shoo the dog away and want sex there a lot. He concentrated in that area, would venture into my bedroom occasionally when the coast seemed clear. There were times that I knew my mother was in the house upstairs when this was occurring—I believe she was completely aware on some level that this was occurring, but was either too indifferent to my situation or did not feel compelled to intervene."

Sometimes, Keith would beat him senseless. That got the old man's rocks off, too.

"I'll never forget the rancid smell of his sweat: cheap hand cream, mingled with acrid smoke of menthol cigarettes he smoked while masturbating. He has a very unusual body mark, or a scar, on the tip of his penis. It was very noticeable when he had an erection and since he frequently stuck it in my mouth, . . . yeah, I got a good look at it. The scar came out of the hole and down the head—just really weird.

"I remember being about age fourteen when this was over, when I had considered castrating myself—I think I had the knife ready and was kind of looking for a way to commit suicide. That summer was rough for me, to say the least. I very nearly did it. But my story took a turn for the better—I met a girl and she showed me that I could be loved. She gave her heart to me and when I was with her, I didn't feel like a freak, I felt good about myself. She was my first love—gets complicated. But, that is the basic narrative."

Michael confronted his parents after his second child was born. He told Keith he could still have contact with his grandsons but he would never be alone with them. As crazy as it sounds, he didn't want to deprive his children of some kind of relationship with his father. Michael's only condition: Keith had to admit to the abuse. His parents cut off all ties with him instead. Then, a few years ago, Keith sent him a card. He claimed he had stage-four colon cancer and probably wouldn't live long.

"Still trying to manipulate me," said Michael. "Still trying to control the situation, find a way to get me back."

* * *

"What side of the fence are you on?" my grandfather asked me on the porch of his house in Alliance that day.

I didn't tell him that my five-month-old daughter inherited his red hair and that I have to think about him every time someone asks about it.

"You need to go away," I said. "Someone should have put you away a long time ago. And I'm going to try now. But I was curious if you'd admit it first."

"I've done some terrible things in my life," he said. "But I'm in the church. I'm doing better. I'm a better man."

"Okay."

"This is a bad time for me," he said.

"Would there be a good time for this story?"

"You don't understand, Jimmy. I just found out I have stage-four colon cancer. I probably don't have much time left."

"Would you do me a favor?" I asked. "Please write down everything you did so we have it when you're dead."

He nodded. "I've written some things already."

After I wrote about my grandfather's crimes, my aunt contacted a police detective and tried to press charges. But Ohio's conservative congress has put restrictions on prosecuting rape cases—you've got to file within twenty years. Here's the thing, though—rapists screw up their victims so much that it usually takes more than twenty years to get healthy enough to talk about it. Even Michael's assaults occurred beyond the twenty-year threshold.

Over those years, Keith had maintained contact with some of his children. And their children. And though they took precautions to protect their own kids, no one in the family believes he ever stopped his predations.

My grandfather exhibited a very special and rare combination of behaviors that are shared by the killers I like to hunt. He's a sexual sadist who enjoys not just the control he has over his victims, but also the physical pain he administers through beatings. He's highly intelligent and organized. And he knows how to manipulate children.

After I wrote a story about the decades of abuse and posted it on my blog, I heard from a number of parishioners from his church. Keith, they told me, was a friendly guy, not the sort who would do something so depraved. Why, he always invited the children to the kitchen in the basement for ice cream after mass.

Sometimes, the best you can do is knock on the monster's door and tell him you know what he did. And then write about it.

FORTY-ONE

Outliers

I have this theory, something I've noticed while studying unsolved abductions and murders: It takes an uncommon mind to commit an uncommon crime. These people, these killers and scoundrels, are outliers, citizens whose routines fall outside society's average behavior.

Example: my favorite suspect in the murder of Amy Mihaljevic. He was a middle school science teacher, but far from "average" in his field. He kept a small zoo in his classroom. He was voted Teacher of the Year. He played ragtime piano. He'd once taken two years off from teaching. For those two years, he wandered the country, working briefly at Disneyland. He had a sister who died of polio when they were prepubescent kids. Nothing about this man's life was average.

Kate Markopoulos, Maura's friend, is an outlier. One of my Irregulars pointed me to some old newspapers from upstate New York, articles that gave Kate a very unique backstory. You see, in

1995, Kate's father tried to blow up his neighbor with a homemade bomb.

This was in Porter Corners, an isolated suburb of Saratoga Springs. The Markopoulos family lived on a private road and shared a driveway with the Finamores, who had a daughter in high school about Kate's age. Daniel, Kate's father, was a hunter who killed game for food. He was also handy with explosives, known for making his own black-powder bombs, which he used to destroy stumps in his backyard. In the winter, Daniel plowed Hall Road for his neighbors. But then he started bickering with Steven Finamore about property lines and the animosity boiled over into Hatfield and McCoy territory.

On September 30, 1995, someone left a bomb with a mercury-switch trigger beside Finamore's garage door. When Steven Finamore picked it up, it exploded in his face. His daughter, Annemarie, found him moments later, covered in blood. The explosion left him blind in one eye and with only partial sight in the other.

At first, Daniel Markopoulos told local reporters he had nothing to do with the explosion, and expressed concern that there might be some madman out there trying to blow people up. But when questioned by state police tech sergeant John Curry, he admitted to making a bomb, though he insisted the one he'd constructed was left in the woods and couldn't be the one that hurt Steve Finamore. Still, Daniel readily admitted that he would have liked to kill Finamore if given the chance.

"As we got in the bomb conversation, he indicated he didn't like Mr. Finamore to the point where he would kill Mr. Finamore, but he would never do it with a bomb," Curry said during testimony.

Judge James Nichols tried to bar reporters from covering the case, stating that he was concerned about the effect the publicity might have on Daniel's daughter Kate, according to articles published in Albany's *Times Union*.

Eventually, Markopoulos pleaded guilty to attempted criminal possession of a dangerous weapon. "Daniel J. Markopoulos single-handedly changed the course of two families' lives," Steven's wife, Diane, said in her victim impact statement. "He never took into account the outcome of his actions, only whatever was in his twisted mind, with no respect to the cost to others, even his own family. He is a liar and a coward." Daniel was sentenced to three to six years in prison, and was released in 2000.

Since our first conversation, I felt that Kate was being evasive about what she knew about the days leading up to Maura's disappearance. She claimed to have forgotten the names of everyone present at the dorm party the night Maura wrecked her father's car. Was the evasiveness I sensed just the fear that someone would uncover this frightening bit of family history?

I called Kate and asked her about all this, gave her another opportunity to explain her strange reactions. "My father didn't do it," was all she said. "He was wrongfully imprisoned."

Not everyone with a shady family history should be looked on with suspicion. My grandfather was one of the most prolific rapists in Ohio. Should his behavior cast a shadow over me? It certainly influenced me, didn't it—I've spent a good part of my life tracking down men just like him. But no, the story of Kate's father didn't prove anything.

Still, it was odd. It was very odd.

FORTY-TWO

More Trouble in St. Albans

I've never been able to track down Kathleen, Maura's older sister, and I'm pretty good at tracking people down. She's an important source. When Maura was found catatonic at Melville Hall, she had muttered, "My sister." Since she had spoken to Kathleen that night, police assumed that "my sister" meant Kathleen and not Julie. When detectives asked Kathleen about the nature of the phone call, she said she had told Maura about a fight with her husband, Tim Carpenter.

A cop in Hanson suggested I make public records requests in northern Vermont, and that's how I eventually found Kathleen's trail.

On the banks of Lake Champlain near the Canadian border is a town called Swanton. It's one of those border towns that can't make up its mind what it wants to be, a mixture of French Canadian, Native American, and rugged U.S.A. mountainmen. I hate places like this. Makes me paranoid. Everything is familiar and yet nothing feels the same.

Swanton is home to a surviving tribe of Abenaki Indians, part of the Algonquin people. A group of Abenaki known as the St. Francis–Sokoki band tried to organize a tribal council here but have not yet been formally recognized by the federal government. There are not many Abenaki left. In the early 1900s, the State of Vermont forcibly sterilized members of their community and terminated the pregnancies of 3,400 Abenaki women. Some would call that genocide. This happened in America, less than a hundred years ago.

Oh, and there's a monster in the lake. Locals call it Champ, or Champie. The Abenaki knew it as Tatoskok. Some believe the animal is a living dinosaur—a plesiosaur, to be exact.

The Abenaki believe our universe is a dream and that words have souls.

This is where Kathleen ended up, living out of a run-down trailer with a man named Harold St. Francis, a descendant of the Abenaki chief. One night in 2011, St. Francis fought with Kathleen and the cops were called. The police who responded were from St. Albans, the nearest sizable community. During the search of their trailer, officers found marijuana plants growing in plastic buckets. They arrested both of them. St. Francis was charged with domestic violence. Kathleen got pinched for cultivation and violation of "pre-trial conditions of release," which meant she had a separate criminal case pending at the time.

She was busted again, a year later, this time for driving drunk on a suspended license. Kathleen's blood-alcohol level at the time of her arrest was .352. That is the highest BAC I've ever heard of. Anything over a .3 carries the risk of death from alcohol poisoning.

At that level, you've gone beyond the point of memory blackout. You will lose control of your bladder whether you like it or not. And you may just stop breathing altogether. A woman Kathleen's size would have to drink ten beers in less than an hour to get that drunk.

The only person I know who drank like that was my grandfather. He used to come home after work and polish off a twelve-pack, one after the other, until it was all gone. It kept his conscience quiet.

As surprised as I was at the depth of her problems, it fit with the stories I had heard. A national television producer once told me that Kathleen was "blackout drunk" when they interviewed her. A cop in Hanson said she and her mother were alcoholics and the rest of the family were "heavy drinkers."

Remember that "fearful symmetry" stuff? Well, here was a doozy. The other woman who disappeared in 2004, Brianna Maitland, worked as a waitress in St. Albans. Brianna had been mixed up with the local drug scene when she vanished. And here was Kathleen, mixed up in the St. Albans drug scene, too.

FORTY-THREE

The Zaps

I stopped taking my meds at the beginning of February. I didn't flush the remaining pills down the toilet, nothing dramatic like that. I had been on Cymbalta for three and a half years and it was time to come off it and see if my body had learned to produce the correct amount of serotonin it needs to regulate my mood. "It's like priming a pump," my psychiatrist, an older Indian man, explained to me. "If we take you off slowly, your body will adjust. It will begin producing the chemicals you need to be well-balanced and happy again." I had already stepped down from sixty milligrams to thirty. And at the beginning of February, I stopped completely.

I understood that I would experience withdrawal. I understood that on an abstract level. I prepared myself for some physical discomfort, but I wasn't really worried.

The first few days after quitting, I experienced unfamiliar clarity. I was suddenly hyperaware of the moment, of the passing of time, of my thoughts and emotions. It was like coming awake after a surgery. I began to have vivid, frightening nightmares. I dreamt I drove to my grandfather's house and shot him with the gun he keeps under his bed. I had the kind of dreams that are so terrible you wake up thinking they're real and that your life has changed for the worst and then you remember it was only a dream and you thank God for that.

About three days in, the zaps started.

The best way I can describe the zaps is that it feels like your soul keeps slipping out of your body, the way a bum vertebra can slip out of alignment with your spine. It felt like an unhinging. Except, this was in my head. And when I say it happened in my head I don't mean that I was imagining it. I mean, physically, this was happening under my skull. It was like someone was reaching into my brain and shocking my frontal lobe with a 9-volt battery.

This started when I was in the car, and it seemed to be connected to the use of my peripheral vision. Whenever I looked at something out of the corner of my eye—ZAP! I thought I might be having a stroke on Route 8, southbound. It was unpleasant, but not as unpleasant as what came next: the crying. The uncontrollable crying.

Commercials are the fucking worst. There was this one where a kid brings his father a box of Cheerios and explains that he should eat this cereal because he wants his dad to be around for a long, long time and Cheerios will help his heart. Yeah. Like a baby, I cried. Songs on the radio: "Fooling Yourself," by Styx. "Blackbird." Anything by the fucking Eagles. Oh, but I loved it. I loved the cries. For years, I had never felt so emotional, so out of control of my feelings. It felt good to cry. It felt good to feel. But it was also scary. Like drinking a cold beer at the end of a hot day after being sober for three years.

Speaking of drinking, I was drinking more. At the time, it

didn't register. But in hindsight, I see how I replaced the Cymbalta with booze. I drank every night. Beer, at first. Miller Lite. Yuengling. Quickly, though, I switched to liquor. I was partial to Bulleit Rye. I kept a bottle of vodka in the freezer. After Julie fell asleep on the couch I would get drunk and stream *Doctor Who*.

About two weeks in, the last of the Cymbalta filtered out of my system and I had a panic attack. I knew, even while it was happening, that this was the last of the withdrawals, my subconscious mind's last attempt to get me to feed it the meds again. It was like the breaker waves around a deserted island, keeping the castaway trapped, the last barrier to the free, empty sea. I sent Julie to her parents' with the kids overnight. I felt dangerous. I went to a movie and sobbed in a dark theater, then went home and drank myself into oblivion. In the morning, my head pulsed with a brown hangover and I felt better.

I was ready to be a good husband and father again. Except that's not how things worked out.

FORTY-FOUR

Silver Linings

It's hard to reconcile my life, how it got so strange while I was deep into the Maura Murray case and going off psychotropic drugs. But here's a for instance: The day that Bradley Cooper was nominated for an Academy Award for his role in *Silver Linings Playbook*, people from his company, along with a screenwriter and a veteran team of producers, walked into Warner Bros. and pitched my novel, *The Man from Primrose Lane*. Deals were made.

It felt like a deus ex machina, like whoever was in charge of the story of my life had gotten lazy and written in a foolish happy ending. It reminded me of that moment in *Return of the King* where Frodo and Sam are about to burn to a crisp on Mount Doom and there's nothing they can do and no one around to save them and then all of the sudden Gandalf flies in on the back of some eagle and saves the day. That's a deus ex machina. It's the writer stepping in and resolving something the characters can't resolve for themselves.

Success really fucks with me. I never trust it. It makes me paranoid. When my book was purchased, I went into a depression for a month. Why? I'm not entirely sure, but I think it has something to do with proving my worth, that if someone thinks I have a modicum of talent, I now have to prove it to them by doing it again. Except, deep inside, I know I'm just a parlor magician, a hack writer who pulled the wool over their eyes just long enough to get a little money out of them. When the Warner Bros. deal happened and my agent explained to me that I would be getting a half-million dollars the day they started principal photography, the first thing I did was picture myself jumping off the Y-Bridge. Let me die for chrissakes before they figure out they wasted all that money.

I was failing as a dad, too. This was becoming obvious.

Casey had been tossed out of his anchor school and was now enrolled at a school for the "behaviorally challenged." More and more often, he was spending time in the "support room." The support room is a section of the school set up like a jail pod: two padded rooms that open into a common area with a bench. The rooms have locks. Now, I can feel some parents cringing. Jail cells in public schools? But we're talking inner-city Akron. And this is their behavioral school. The kids are here because they are a danger to other students. In a typical K-12 setting, a kid acts the way these kids do, they'd be sent to juvie. I think most parents would prefer to send their kids to the support room for ten minutes instead of juvie jail for a night. There's a cop on duty at all times, to protect the teachers.

That being said, every time I heard Casey was in the support room, I'd get angry. Angry at his teachers for putting him in there and not being able to deal with a goddamn kindergartener, angry with Casey for not acclimating to school, to life.

Time-outs didn't work anymore. There was nothing left. So we went back to spanking.

I should have known how he'd react; it's what I did, after all. When I spanked Casey, he found that calm place I had discovered. That calmness on the other side of rage. I would spank him and then he'd smile. He'd fucking smile at me and say, "That didn't hurt," like he was a young Giles Corey.

We fed off each other's madness, two mirrors facing each other, an endless loop of anger. Each day he got worse and so did I. How far could we push each other to get some kind of reaction? Never mind that he was five and I was thirty-five. I couldn't let him win. I couldn't give him that control.

One night at the end of February, he threw water in my face and I spanked him. "That didn't hurt," he said, smiling. So I spanked him, harder. And he cried. And a bit of my heart broke.

I went back on the Cymbalta and never spanked my kid again. Fuck it. I'd rather I spoil him more and have him end up in juvie because I wasn't hard enough on him as a kid than risk hurting him. As my highs and lows were cut off by the drugs again, Casey started doing better at school. He stopped fighting with us. My calmness was infecting him, just as his rage had infected me.

I am the potential cancer in my son's genetic code. I am a decent man. But I could have gone the other way. If my mother had not shown me kindness, I could have been really dangerous. I feel it in my bones. And let's not beat around the bush: These mysteries I write about, they serve a very specific purpose, don't they? They fulfill an obsessive need to understand violence, a compulsion to hunt. I hunt the bad guys. But, if things had gone just a bit differently . . .

I have to make sure Casey becomes a decent man. And if pills help, so what?

Sometimes a deus ex machina is a pill.

J. R. R. Tolkien didn't care that some critics viewed his eagles as bad writing. He knew enough about the world, the violent world of wars and murder, to know that there is always hope. He even had a word for it. Here's how he explained it:

"I coined the word 'eucatastrophe': the sudden happy turn in a story which pierces you with a joy that brings tears. And I was there led to the view that it produces its peculiar effect because it is a sudden glimpse of Truth; your whole nature, chained in material cause and effect, the chain of death, feels a sudden relief as if a major limb out of joint had suddenly snapped back."

FORTY-FIVE

Confrontations

Julie Murray is a spook, but she was easier to find than Kathleen. After graduating from West Point, Maura's older sister got a job at Booz Allen, a defense contractor recently in the news for having employed Edward Snowden. The NSA contracted with Booz Allen for a series of clandestine jobs involving the mass surveillance of American citizens. Snowden blew the whistle, alerting the general public to this Orwellian invasion of privacy, and has been on the run ever since. By 2013, Julie Murray was working as an executive officer for the Department of Defense. I found her living out of a modest apartment not far from Booz Allen's headquarters, near D.C.

This was near the end of March. I had decided to return to New England to interview Maura's close friends and family, the ones who never returned my messages. Many of them had gone to great lengths to hide their home addresses. But my good friend

Mike Lewis, who runs Confidential Investigative Services, one of Cleveland's top private eye agencies, tracked them down for me. Julie was first on my list.

Her apartment was in a historic three-story with a state-of-the-art intercom system. As I arrived, an older woman who lived in the complex invited me in. I climbed the stairs to Julie's apartment. I knocked. Heavy footsteps walked to the door but the door did not open. I listened. A television played softly in the background. Then, from the other side of the door came a low growl, the sort of guttural growl only very large dogs can make. It sounded like a mastiff or something. Quickly, I walked back down to the lobby and sat on a bench. I figured I'd wait a bit to see if Julie or her boyfriend walked by. It was just after five on a Friday afternoon.

I didn't have to wait long. The back door opened a half hour later and Julie came inside, followed by a tall, well-dressed black man.

"Julie?" I asked. "Julie Murray?"

"Yes?" She was immediately apprehensive and her companion stepped in front of her.

"I'm James Renner," I said, extending my hand. "I'd like to ask you a couple questions about Maura."

She shook my hand before the name really registered, then she pulled her hand back, quickly. "How did you get in?"

"A neighbor let me in."

"Who?" the black man asked.

I shrugged.

"How did you find out where we live?" he asked. "We're unlisted."

God, his voice sounded familiar.

"I found it from your voter records."

"Bullshit," he said.

The man on the telephone! He sounded exactly like the man who had called me years ago, when I was just beginning to look into Maura's disappearance, the guy who'd called me and said there was information that should be released. He had promised to get his girlfriend to call me, but I'd never heard from either of them again. Was it him?

"I just want to ask a couple questions," I said. "I tried to contact you on Facebook. I left messages."

"That was four years ago," she said.

Jesus. *Four years.* "Was it really that long ago?"

She nodded.

"Julie, what was Fred doing in Amherst the weekend before Maura disappeared? He wasn't really there to help Maura look for a car, was he? What was he doing there with four thousand dollars in cash?"

"Don't," the man said. "Don't say anything."

"Why not?" I asked.

"This is all going to end up on your blog," Julie said.

"You need to leave," the man said. "I'm going to go get my dogs if you don't leave."

"Why won't you let her talk? You can see she wants to say something."

"I'm an attorney," he said.

"Good to know." I turned back to Julie, who was now looking back and forth at us, as if she was waiting to see who would take the first swing.

"I can tell you exactly why my dad was there," she said.

"Julie," the man shouted. "Don't say anything more. Don't say another word to this man."

"I told the police," she offered. "I told the police everything. But I don't think I could tell you. It's an open investigation."

"Help me out, Julie," I said.

"Get out of here or I'm calling the police," the man said.

"Okay, do that," I said.

"I can tell you, finding my sister is still the number one priority," Julie said. "That's number one. Nothing else matters. None of that other stuff matters."

"What other stuff?"

"I don't like the things you've written about my father."

"Julie!" the man said.

"What things?"

"Was my father a hard-ass? Yes. Did he drive us hard? Yes. Is he the best father a girl could have?" She paused. Then said, "Yes."

"Julie," the man said. He put a hand on her back and directed her to the stairs.

"I'm calling the police," he said.

My next stop was Sara Alfieri. Sara had hosted the dorm party the night Maura wrecked her father's car. She had never returned my e-mails or calls. Sara keeps an unlisted number and lives in the greater Boston area, where she works as a staff accountant for Trip-Advisor.

It was dark by the time I knocked on her door. Her response when I introduced myself was complete shock. I have never seen someone react so viscerally to a drop-in, and I've dropped in on serial killers. She blanched. "How did you find me?"

"What happened the night of the party, Sara?"

"I can't talk about that!" she yelled. She slammed the door. I left my number, but she never called.

It was what I expected, but I am still confounded by the way

Maura's friends and family have shut out the media. This is a missing-persons case. Most families of a missing person would kill to have this kind of attention. Not the Murrays. Not Maura's friends. At some point, you have to start asking, Why?

FORTY-SIX

"Drunk and Naked"

The next day, I popped in on two of Maura's childhood friends, Liz Drewniak and Katie Jones. In both cases, their husbands came to the door and told me that the women didn't have anything to say. They were nice enough about it. Liz, her husband told me, is trying to distance herself emotionally from Maura Murray's disappearance and its aftermath. Katie had just returned from the hospital and was laid up in bed with the new baby. Months later, I received a brief e-mail from her:

> I just wanted to write to you and say thank you for your work on Maura's case and that I am sorry I haven't contacted you in the past. . . . Of course I would love answers to this mystery as much as everyone else. Unfortunately I think you know everything and probably more than I do at this point. . . .

As I left Katie's house, Mike Lewis, the private eye, e-mailed me another dossier. Out of curiosity, he'd run a background check on Maura. Something odd popped up. Someone had used Maura's social security number in Saco, Maine, in October of 2004, eight months after she disappeared.

My next stop was the house in Hanover that Maura's sister, Kathleen, had once shared with Tim Carpenter. When I arrived at the modest split-level, I found a construction crew breaking for lunch. They were busy remodeling the place. The owner was there. Said she got the property for a steal but it was turning into a lot of work. No, she didn't know where I could find Kathleen. Heard she'd gotten into some trouble.

The guy next door was more help. "Don't know where Kathleen is," he said. "But Tim's at work, right here in town. You could probably catch him."

"Where?"

The town council calls it a "transfer station," but everyone else just calls it the dump. Tim was wearing a fluorescent vest, directing traffic to the smasher. The smasher is in a concrete ditch about six feet across and thirty long. People put their trash in there and then a giant stainless-steel piston smashes everything flat.

My first impression of Tim Carpenter was that he was the sort of guy who'd seen hard living. Tragically skinny. Thin, long face; patchy beard. Based on looks, he was the kind of guy who'd deck you for saying, "Hi." But once he started talking, I was taken by his levity, his carefree old-hippie attitude, that openness you get from surviving hard times.

He started at the beginning. And I mean the beginning. Turns out Tim was adopted, born at the Elizabeth Lund Home for Unwed Mothers up in Burlington. He was part Blackfoot Indian, he said, which explained the stories his neighbors had about the tepee he built in his backyard. He'd met Kathleen when she was still living in Hanson, next door to his parents' place. He seems unconcerned with the question of love. It was a relationship. It happened. There were good times. It ended.

They were both into drinking and drugs, he said. But he got sober and she didn't. "I took her to detox in Branson. That's where she met that St. Francis fellow. Couldn't keep away from him, after."

"Help me with some answers," I said.

Most of what he had to say concerned the weeks after Maura vanished. Tim and Kathleen had driven up to Wells River right away to help Fred with the search.

"He was weird about it," said Tim. "Me, if it was my daughter, I'da been outside at the crack of dawn, starting the searches every damn day. Him, he'd get up maybe 10 A.M. and I'd say, 'We better get started.' Then he'd stop about 5 P.M. and bring everyone to the restaurant and start drinking and it would be a party."

Tim felt that, when the media was around, Fred would put on a show, act manic, like they had to find her right now, right fucking now. But as soon as the cameras were gone, he'd slow up and go back to normal, Tim said.

Later, Fred asked Tim to drive his truck to Maura's dorm. By the time they got there, Fred had put everything Maura left—a computer, clothes—into boxes. They loaded the stuff into Tim's flatbed and from there, everything went into his closet in Hanover. Fred was not interested in picking through the material for clues, so Tim let another guy, a volunteer named Rick, look through it to see if he could find anything interesting.

"There was something Fred said once that made the hair on the back of my neck stand up," said Tim. "I remember him pointing up to the mountain and saying, 'She walked up there. We'll find her at the top. Drunk and naked.'"

The last he'd heard, Kathleen was still living up in Swanton or St. Albans. Maybe homeless.

We were wrapping up, so I asked Tim a tough question about Fred. He thought for a couple seconds, then nodded. "Twice, Kathleen got blackout drunk and said something about it," he said. "But it was never something I asked about when she was sober."

After that conversation I drove directly to Hanson, hoping to catch Fred himself, at his old house. But he wasn't there. He's lived on the Cape for some time now. I knew that. But Fred, Jr., was home. I told him what Tim had told me.

"Never happened," he said, standing in the doorway. "You know what? I want to reach out and strangle you right now. But I know you're goading me. You want me to kick your ass. That would make a good scene in your book."

On my way to Swanton, somewhere along Route 91 northbound, Tim called me.

"I thought of something else," he said. "That guy Rick, the guy who was helping us out? You should talk to him. His name's Rick Graves." He gave me the man's number, and I recognized the area code right away.

"Wait. This number isn't Massachusetts," I said. "Where's this guy from?"

"Saco, Maine," said Tim.

FORTY-SEVEN

Graves

"I was hip to hip with Fred on those searches up in New Hampshire," said Graves when I got him on the horn. He was forty years old in 2004, working at Home Depot, measuring floors, when he heard about Maura's disappearance. Graves was a searcher—that's what he did for fun, searched for stuff. Not just people, but downed planes or anything that was lost. He'd gone searching for a Learjet that crashed into a mountain around that time. When he saw a news story on TV about Maura, he figured he'd drive down and help. He went with a friend named David Lachance, a self-taught dowser.

They found Fred at the Wells River Motel. The family was glad to have the extra help, he said. Graves rented a room and began to explore the woods around Haverhill for Maura's body. Every weekend for a year Graves drove to New Hampshire, then every other week the following year. "It takes you over," he explained. "It was my whole life for three years."

Tim and Kathleen helped with the searches, too. So did
Fred's cousins Sookie and Patti. It worked like this: In the morn-
ings, Fred would go jogging, then return to the motel to shower.
After that, Fred would give everyone "leads" and they would break
into small groups to go scouting. The immediate area around
where Maura was last seen was heavily searched.

Though they never found a body, they did, occasionally, find
odd things. Graves found an empty vodka bottle on Lime Kiln
Road, not far from the crash, but nothing ever came of it. Once,
Fred and Kathleen discovered a pair of thong underwear in a driveway. But the cops said it wasn't Maura's. "Me, I think it might have
been hers," Graves said. Then there was the time he found a trash
bag full of blood and hair in the woods. Everyone got really excited for a while, but the remains turned out to be a deer.

Days like that took a toll on everyone. Sometimes Graves
would call his girlfriend back in Maine and tell her he was never
going to come back to Haverhill, that he was done. But he always
returned the next weekend.

At the end of each day, everyone would meet back at the motel and then go out to eat. Fred always paid the bill. "I offered
once," said Graves, "but he wasn't having it."

Graves said Fred was decent enough, considering the circumstances. "I took psychology," he said. "I know good people and I
know bad people. Fred is conservative. He only talks to who he
wants to talk to."

Fred gave him special assignments, like handling all the psychics who called. Graves also wrote up the Freedom of Information request that Fred used to launch his legal battle against the
State of New Hampshire. And Fred allowed Graves to put a trace
on Maura's social security number, which is why his address in
Saco dinged on my P.I.'s background check.

Locals often stopped by the motel to share tips with them, some of which they forwarded to police. One big lead was about a red truck seen near the crash the night of Maura's disappearance. Someone got the license plate number and Graves was able to trace it back to a local man. But nobody ever talked to him.

In the boxes from Maura's dorm, Graves found a few notes to Billy. He discovered that Maura was contacting brewpubs all around Massachusetts, looking for a job. But there was no smoking gun in all that junk, he said.

Looking back, Graves believes something of great importance happened at that party the night Maura wrecked her father's car on the way to his hotel.

"We heard a lot of rumors about that party," he said. "We never got everything out of Kate or Sara. We never figured out who else was there. I think one of them knows something."

Graves had some tough questions for Fred, too. Such as why he sometimes lied to the media. The story Fred told Graves didn't line up with the story in the newspapers about the night of that party. "When Maura drove to his motel that night, the manager called Fred's room and told him to come to the lobby. Fred told me that when he got there, he found Maura slumped over in a chair, crying. He never told me what she was crying about. And I never pushed him. One guy you don't want to push is Fred Murray. He'll clam up and never talk to you again."

One afternoon, Graves drove into Hanover to pick up Tim. Fred was there. But Fred didn't want to talk to Graves, Tim told him. Fred didn't even want to see him. "I haven't talked to him since," said Graves. "That was a real kick in the ass, you know? He just wants it left alone now. I think he just wants to be at peace."

FORTY-EIGHT

Borderland

On my way to St. Albans in search of Kathleen Murray, I stopped for a bite and to check my e-mail. Several Irregulars alerted me to an official statement that had just been released by Maura's siblings and posted to the Maura Murray Facebook page. My recent conversation with Fred, Jr., had drawn a response.

> Over the past couple of years, a number of people have decided that personal gain by making unsubstantiated claims is more important than the fact a young girl is missing and a family is left shattered, still seeking answers. Maura's story is not a fictitious account dreamed up by a script writer. Instead, it is an actual case that still needs answers. Painting a story based upon conjecture and allegations, as well as sensationalizing to meet some Hollywoodistic standard, seem more important to some than a bonafide effort to help us discover Maura's

whereabouts. Recently, outrageous and completely false allegations vilifying our father and our family have surfaced during this difficult time. While some may give instant credibility to these allegations, there is never a mention of any investigation to determine the presence of any biases or motives to fabricate of these sources. We feel all sources of information, along with any persons of interest, should endure the same level of scrutiny to determine if derogatory facts exist which may call their credibility into question. We remain a united family struggling with the unconscionable burden of a missing loved one, a burden that we wish upon no one. Each and every day our family lives and relives this tragedy, the weight of which has affected us all, none more so than our father. We remain steadfast in our efforts to find our sister, and we thank all of those who have provided and continue to provide love and support along this difficult road.

Regards,
Kathleen, Freddie, Julie and Kurtis

That letter stung. It did. It made me feel just like the sleazy reporter they make me out to be. I'm used to this kind of reaction from the families of murder *suspects*. But coming from the family of the person I was trying to find was a slap in the face. What bothered me most was the easy argument that I was out for personal gain.

By that time, I had spent over $500 on public records. I had traveled to New England four times. During each of those trips, I paid for hotels and food and gas. I had yet to receive even an advance on the book. My time would have been better spent writing a new novel.

I found it curious that Fred had not signed the letter.

Confused as ever, I got back in my car and drove north.

There is something wrong with Swanton. There's some darkness in the musty breeze rolling off Lake Champlain, in the low-lying gray clouds, the brick-front downtown slanted against the main road. This place is American. Americana. The Dam Furniture Store with its hand-painted sign; the Swanton House of Pizza by the curve down to the Missisquoi River. It doesn't feel right. None of it. The edge of Canada is within sight. Directly north is the part of Canada that is decidedly French, home of the Québécois. So yes, Swanton is part of the United States, but there's something foreign about the place. In the architecture. In the lilting of the words from the mouths of strangers. There is no cultural anchor here, and the effect is disconcerting.

My iPhone cut out on 91. Without GPS, I had to cruise around a bit before I found Jonergin Drive. Kathleen had lived in a blue trailer here. I arrived at night and no one was home. I struck up a conversation with the family next door. The man was cleaning his boat and invited me inside. His wife told me that she remembered Kathleen, that she'd been one of "St. Francis's girls," but she hadn't seen her in a while. St. Francis was gone, too.

I grabbed a room at a cheap motel down the road. It was little more than a flophouse, and bitter cold when I entered. It took ten minutes for the industrial wall heater to wake up the room. I got up early and made my way to a greasy-spoon diner on the other side of town. Gnomini was waiting for me inside.

I'd never met any of my Irregulars before. "Gnomini" often posted on Websleuths, and was one of the frequent readers who helped me now and then. Turned out he was a former reporter, retired and hard of hearing. After breakfast, I got into his car so he could drive me to another address we'd found for Kathleen. As we drove across the train tracks, I thought again about how eager, apparently, I was to get into strange men's cars. I didn't know this man. Not really. He was no more than an online avatar to me. He could kill me and bury me and nobody would ever know. Is that what I wanted? I was beginning to suspect that maybe it was.

The address we had turned out to be the probation office in St. Albans. That's where Kathleen's mail was being forwarded.

Gnomini took me back to the diner and then, on a whim, I drove by the trailer on Jonergin, where Kathleen had lived with St. Francis, one more time. A man was inside, ripping out the walls and throwing everything onto the lawn. I parked on the shoulder and walked over, knocked on the open door.

"Just bought the place," he told me after I introduced myself. "Gonna gut it and fix it up, rent it out."

I asked him if he'd found anything interesting while cleaning.

"Needles, man," he said. "Fucking needles everywhere."

FORTY-NINE

I Saw Your Think

"I have to tell you about something that happened with Casey," Julie said shortly after I returned home. Normally, when my wife said something like this, it wasn't good. But this was different, I could tell. Julie didn't look sad; she looked excited and maybe a little scared.

"What is it?" I asked.

"Well. We're sitting at the table, having dinner. And I was thinking about what I would pack him for lunch tomorrow. And I thought to myself, *I'll make him a salami sandwich; I bet he'd like that.* I'd never made him a salami sandwich before but then I thought it, that I would. And then he looks at me and says, 'Yes. I'd like a salami sandwich for lunch. You could pack it in my bag.'"

Something you should know about my wife. She is a skeptic to the nth degree. She was raised Catholic but was never confirmed because she didn't believe. When pressed, she'll call herself an agnostic, but she's really an atheist, or damn close. She doesn't believe in UFOs. She doesn't believe in Bigfoot. Doesn't believe in ghosts.

"Do you think he read your mind?" I asked.

She shrugged. "I asked him why he said it and then he said, 'Mom, I can see your think.'"

"'Your think'?"

"Like a balloon or something above my head. Like a thought balloon from a comic strip."

It became a cute running joke for us, this phrase "I can see your think." But it happened again and again, with increasing regularity.

On the way to soccer practice, he asked me who would coach his team that day.

"What do you mean?" I asked. "The coach, of course."

He looked troubled. "What if she's sick?"

"She's never been too sick for practice before," I assured him.

When we got there, a man we didn't recognize was gathering up the kids. The coach had called in sick.

The defining moment for me happened at Wal-Mart. I took Casey to return a birthday present. We were in line at Customer Service behind a quiet, elderly woman. Casey began to sing, "Just thinkin' about, tomorrow . . ."

The woman kind of jumped and looked around at my son. Something had terrified her. But all he was doing was singing this song from *Annie*. I thought it was maybe a little weird, since we hadn't seen that movie in like six months and he was singing it out of the blue, but so what?

As she was leaving, the woman stopped next to me. She seemed to consider whether or not to say anything, and then finally she said, "I've had that song stuck in my head since yesterday. The one your son starting singing. I think he picked it out of my head."

"He likes that movie," I said by way of explanation.

But she shook her head. "He didn't start it at the beginning. He started it right where I was in the song and sang along with me in my head. And now it's gone."

It was early April and I was driving Casey to school, with Lainey in her car seat.

"Do you want to go to jail?" he asked.

"What? No," I said. "Why would you ask that?"

He just shrugged. But I could see his face in the rearview, and he looked troubled. He looked the way he'd looked when he knew his coach was sick.

FIFTY

Eucatastrophe

May sixth. I was sitting with the other parents in the lobby of Flytz Gym in Cuyahoga Falls, waiting for Casey to finish tumbling class, when I got the first text:

Amanda and Gina just walked out of a house on the West Side, was all it said.

"Holy shit," I said, out loud. Some of the other parents looked at me with concern. I ignored them. A miracle had happened in Cleveland, and soon they would hear it for themselves. A collective "Holy shit!" was about to echo out from Northeast Ohio and travel across the world. Amanda Berry and Gina DeJesus had just returned from the dead. They were alive! *Together.* After all this time.

Then another text: *There's a third woman here.*

"Holy shit," I said again.

A woman crinkled her nose at me.

As soon as practice ended, I drove Casey home. I dropped

him off and explained to Julie what was happening. The news channels didn't have it yet, but they would soon. I wanted to be in Cleveland when it broke. I had to be up there for this. I took the Vibe and jetted north up 77. By the time I was out of Akron, the first radio bulletins were coming in.

Amanda Berry and Gina DeJesus are alive. Another woman, Michelle Knight, was rescued, too, missing for over ten years. Suspect in custody. Nobody dead.

It's one of those stories that's too good to be true. Something so good and full of grace it causes you to reevaluate how you see the world, the reverse of that feeling we felt in our hearts the morning of 9/11. It was Tolkien's *eucatastrophe,* made real. Only, in this story, instead of eagles the deus ex machina was a black man named Charles Ramsey, who pulled Amanda out of that evil house, and who spoke in earnest bon mots: "I knew something was wrong when a little, pretty white girl runs into a black man's arms."

As I drove for Cleveland, I wondered who the suspect could be. Could he be the boogeyman responsible for all the other unsolved abductions in the area? Was it the man who took Amy Mihaljevic? How much closure could this one day bring?

Instead of driving to the crime scene on Seymour Avenue, I chose to head to MetroHealth Medical Center, where the victims had been transported. I parked my car out front by the media trucks. Every local station was there. Reporters milled about the front portico, waiting for the first official press conference. I jogged past them like I knew what I was doing. A guard let me in the door without questioning me. I was wearing a suit. He probably thought I was a lawyer.

I sat in the reception area, leaned against a wall, and busied myself on my laptop, watching people come and go. About forty-five minutes after I arrived, Gina's mother came in the back. She recognized me from when I worked on her daughter's story and gave me a hug.

"I'm so happy for you," I said.

"I can't believe it," she said. "I . . . I just can't believe it."

A large woman in uniform stepped between us, a liaison with the Cleveland Police Department. "How'd you get in?" she asked.

"I'm not a reporter," I said. "Not anymore, anyway."

"What are you doing here?"

"Someone needs to tell the family how bad this is about to get," I said. I pointed at the glass doors, at the circus setting up outside. "That's just the local media. In an hour, you'll have CNN out there. Fox News. NBC. Probably Nancy Grace. Everyone will want this, and you have to take control of it and set the terms before it gets crazy. The families need a media liaison. But they should do it together."

I gave her my number and asked her to pass it along. My brief intervention probably didn't change anything—the crisis management firms were already reaching out to the families by then, I'm sure. But the women did what I proposed. They united behind a local firm, Hennes Paynter, and successfully weathered the storm of the media onslaught. Of course, after surviving Ariel Castro, the stalker reporters were nothing to fear.

That name: Ariel Castro. Soon as I heard it, I felt my stomach tumble out of my body. I knew that name: Castro. I knew I knew it.

At home, I went through my old notes and e-mails from the months I spent researching Amanda and Gina's disappearance. There it was. Castro. Gina's father had given me the name of Ariel's daughter, Arlene Castro. I'd meant to interview her, but because she was a juvenile, my editor and I had agreed to leave her alone.

What if I had spoken to her? Would she have said something to cast suspicion on her father?

It was exactly two weeks later that I got the call from my mother. I could tell by her tone that something was wrong, really wrong. "Jimmy," she said. "A man is stalking your sister." I listened, and as she talked, I felt that quiet rage turn my blood to ice.

FIFTY-ONE

Contempt

It took me three tries to get the phone number right. Julie answered on the second ring.

"Where are you?" I asked.

"In the car," she said. "With Casey and Lainey."

"Can you pull over?"

"Why?"

"I need you to write something down and I don't want you to get into an accident."

"What's going on?"

"Just pull over."

"I'm in a driveway. What?"

"I need you to call a lawyer named Roger Synenberg."

"What? Why?"

"I'm in jail," I said.

* * *

Let's jump back a bit. There're some things you should know before we get into this.

My mom. She lived in a house on the nice side of Lakewood, with three of my sisters. Barb, the middle one at twenty-two, shared the first floor with our mother. Barb had two dogs, one of which was an American Bulldog, a beast of an animal. I had been trying to talk her into getting rid of it for the better part of the year. Barb reminds me of Maura in many ways and I often asked her for perspective on this mystery as it progressed. She was athletic, like Maura, attractive, quiet. Supersmart, but struggling in college. Studied nursing. Knew her way around bars.

The trouble started when her bulldog attacked another dog outside her house. The dog's owner filed a report and an animal control officer came to the house. He was a young man, Barb's age. Skinny guy, squinty eyes; let's call him Brian. After that first meeting, Brian inserted himself into my sister's life in increasingly odd ways. He started dropping by the house, calling her on the phone. Funny thing, though: Every time he visited, every time he called, he made a point to tell Barb that he was "off duty" and the visits were "not official business." This behavior escalated over several weeks. When Barb didn't answer his calls, Brian called our mother at work to ask where she was. Then he showed up at the house again and told Barb to let him inside so he could look around the first floor. What he was doing was way beyond the scope of his powers. My first thought when I heard all this was that this man was casing the place.

My mind is an encyclopedia of deviant behavior, and Brian's actions reminded me of Dennis Rader—BTK—the serial killer who terrorized Wichita, Kansas, from 1974 until 2005. Rader worked as an animal control officer and used that position to gain information about his victims: whether they had a guard dog; the layout of their homes.

Our mother caught Brian outside the house a few days before she called me. He was out of uniform. He told her that he happened to be walking down their street, off duty, because he lived in the area. But when I ran his background, I found he lived in Westlake, two towns over.

Barb was due in court to answer questions about the dog that day, a Monday. I left the kids with the babysitter and drove up to the Lakewood muni building and got my first look at Brian as he walked into the courtroom. The young man gave me the heebie-jeebies. He sat ten feet from my sister, and leered at her.

The judge came in: Judge Patrick Carroll, an old, cantankerous judge with a reputation for busting chops. He was particularly harsh on drunk drivers.

When he called Barb's name, I escorted her around the partition.

"Who are you?" the judge asked.

"I'm her brother."

"If you're not a lawyer, you can't be here."

"I know," I said. "But there's something going on that you need to hear about."

"Let me ask you again. Are you a lawyer?"

"No."

"Then get out."

I turned to Barb then, realizing, a little late, that this was not going to work out in our favor. Not there. Not then. "Just plead not guilty," I said. "We'll come back."

"Out!"

A police officer who had been standing by the door stepped toward me. I put up my hands to let him know I was leaving. But as I went, I made myself heard. "That man," I said, pointing to the animal control officer where he sat by the prosecutor, "is stalking my sister. Somebody needs to check him out."

I was at the door by the time the judge gave me the ultimatum. "If you say one more word, I will find you in contempt."

It felt like someone had thrown open a door inside my mind. *CREEEK!* Out comes the rage monster. My mind was a whir of memories. What did I know about Judge Carroll? What could I say that would make the most impact, show him how much contempt I really did have for him. Ah yes. The one thing you could never call Judge Carroll . . .

"You're just a drunk!" I shouted. An audible gasp went around the room. I turned my back on him and walked out the door.

The officer by the door was a young fellow by the name of Anthony Ciresi. He'd just escorted a man from jail. That's why he was there. Ciresi followed me out of the courtroom and then threw me across the hall, hard, into the concrete wall. I lost my breath. Couldn't breathe.

I had two distinct thoughts.

Thought one: *Oh shit. The rage is still in control. Wait. Wait. Give me a second to calm down.*

Thought two: *Okay, asshole. You want to fight? Good. Because I've been waiting for a long time to fight someone and you'll do just fine.*

I felt hands on my wrists. I spun, grabbed Ciresi's arm, and flipped him away from me. It was like tossing a bail of hay off a truck. I looked down at him as he picked himself up off the tiled floor, saw the fear in his eyes. Loved it. Loved it if nothing more than for the fact that for the rest of his career, when he feels like roughing up a perp, he'll remember me and how easily I got the drop on him.

I was ready to pounce. I wanted a few swings at that smooth face before anyone could interrupt us. But that other part of me, that newer part of me, that part that is a father and a lover, stepped forward and spoke up: *Don't make it worse!*

It gave Ciresi time to reach his belt. He pulled a weapon. At first I thought it was a gun. But then I noticed that it was bright yellow. A Taser. It was aimed at my heart.

I raised my hands. "Okay," I said.

"Turn around," he growled.

I complied. In a moment, he was cuffing my wrists, digging into the skin as far as it would give, pushing my face against the wall. I turned my head and saw a woman sitting in the hallway, waiting to pay a bill. She'd seen everything, the only witness. Her mouth was open in a comical look of shock. I smiled, tried to look friendly. "Did you see him throw me into the wall?" I asked.

She nodded.

"I'll need your name," I said.

Ciresi pulled me around and marched me down the hall, around the corner, toward the police station on the other side of the building. Other officers were running toward us, in response to the sound of the fight in the hallway. They slowed down when they saw I was cuffed. A couple of cops clapped Ciresi on the back and said odd things such as, "Like father like son." I would discover later that Ciresi was actually the son of the guy who'd run the Lakewood Police Department's detective bureau for many years. Dumb fucking luck.

"I'm not some drunk piece of white trash," I said, trying my best to put the Hulk away, lock that door up before I got myself in deeper. "What you did back there is called 'excessive force.'"

"That right?"

"You're going to be writing parking tickets in a month," I said.

He sighed and wrote something down in his notepad. I had picked the worst thing to say, again.

They charged me with "Assault on a Peace Officer," a felony of the fourth degree. Eighteen months in prison, if convicted. I was given one call, which I used to reach Julie. After that, I was assigned an orange shirt and pants. Someone handed me a bedroll. Another officer escorted me to my cell.

I lay down on the mattress and replayed the events of the day in my mind, tried to figure out just how much trouble I was in. There were about eight other dudes in the jail with me, sitting in the common area, watching TV. They wanted to know what I was in for, but I wouldn't talk to them. I was going to be out soon. I knew I would. I didn't belong there, with them. I pulled the door to my cell shut and locked myself inside.

FIFTY-TWO

Hard Time

"Geez. When he told you to say one more thing, you really made it count," said Dominic Coletta. We were in one of those movie trope situations: me in orange scrubs, behind a pane of plexiglass, speaking into a dirty phone, the lawyer on the other side in a nice suit. When Julie called Roger, Roger had called Dominic. He was a rising star in the world of Cleveland defense lawyers, Roger's protégé. Thin, handsome, dark hair, Italian. He had an economy of words, already.

"Here's the deal, James," he said. "I'm going to get you out of here but it's not going to be today. In the morning, we'll go in front of Judge Carroll. You'll apologize. *Profusely.* And then you'll plead guilty to contempt. There's no wiggle room there. You'll plead guilty and he'll sentence you to some jail time. But that's not what you should be concerned about. Our concern is the felony. They'll have to indict you in Cuyahoga County. But we need to keep you out of county lockup. You don't want to end up there. You want to do your time in a muni jail."

"Okay."

"Where do you work?"

"I'm a special instructor at the University of Akron."

"You'll probably lose your job if you end up with a felony on your record, right?"

"Yes."

"Okay. How many kids?"

I held up two fingers.

"Good. We're gonna get you out of here," he said again.

"One more thing," I said. "I need my Cymbalta. Soon. I can't go through withdrawals in here."

I found a dog-eared copy of Dan Brown's early novel *Deception Point* in the common area and brought it back to my cell. I'd always wanted to read it. Finally had the time. I lay down on the bed and got into it.

A while later, a man came with dinner on one of those industrial school trays. Dry chicken nuggets, bread, corn. A plate of carbs. I didn't touch it. Gave it to the other guys, who were grateful enough for the extra food that they stopped harassing me.

Around nine o'clock, I remembered that I hadn't given Julie instructions about where to pick up Lainey's prescription. She'd been sick for a couple days and her doctor wanted to give her something for her cough. I pressed the button next to the intercom on the wall above the steel toilet.

"Yeah?" came a gruff male voice.

"I have to make a call."

"That right?" he said, and laughed. "I'll get right on that."

He never let me make that call.

It was beginning to sink in: I was in control of nothing.

*   *   *

In the morning, I was brought in front of Judge Carroll. This time I wore an orange suit. Julie and Barb sat in the back of the courtroom.

"I'm sorry," I told the judge. "I'm embarrassed at how I acted. I'm not sure how it all happened."

He didn't look at me. I was sentenced to ten days, an exorbitant sentence for a simple contempt of court. But I'd made it personal.

The cop at my cuffs let me kiss Julie on the way out. I told her I was sorry. And then they returned me to my cell. I sat on the bed and cried and when I was done crying I read. I slept and read. That night I paid the felony bond and around midnight they transferred me to a new jail in the suburbs. "It's the Hilton of local jails," the police officer who drove me there said. "Best place to do time in Cuyahoga County."

They gave me my own room, a narrow concrete stall with a thin bed and a stainless-steel toilet/sink combo. It had a drinking fountain, too, but it wouldn't stop running until you flushed the toilet again. From 7 A.M. to 11 P.M. my door was unlocked and I could sit in a common area that had a TV, a pay phone, and a shower. Two other rooms opened onto this space. For most of the time I was there, it was just me and two other guys in the pod.

Casey was overcurious, as always. I talked to him every night, using the collect-call phone when the other guys were napping. "Did the handcuffs hurt? Is your bed scratchy? Mom says the bed's scratchy and your clothes are itchy. I told the dentist that you were in jail. How long are you going to be in jail?"

We decided not to keep any of this from him, to be entirely truthful about the experience. Our hope was that maybe he would find it a little scary and want to do better in school, that seeing what happens when you fight as an adult would motivate him to stop fighting with his teachers.

"I'm going to get you out," he said, his voice sounding far older than five. "I'll bring a hundred other Caseys and we'll get a ladder and a saw and we'll bust you out!"

"Casey, please don't do anything like that," I said.

"I love you, Dad."

"I love you. To the moon and back."

I noticed the shakes the second morning in the new jail. I couldn't rest my left hand. It wasn't until the migraine started behind my right eye that I understood what was happening. Even though they'd given me the Cymbalta, I was going through withdrawals. I'd been drinking more than I'd realized. Looking back on it, I can see how it happened, gradually: a beer at the end of the day, then two, then a few more and a whiskey chaser. Every night. For something like five months. And, to be completely candid, I'd started dipping into the bottle of oxycodone Julie kept after childbirth. Every other night for a while. Weed. NyQuil, too.

It was a rough twenty-four hours. I stayed in my room and hid under the wool blanket and pretended to sleep.

Out by the TV, the other two inmates (both on thirty-day stretches) watched *Cops* and played cards.

When I woke the next day, I felt a little better. I took a shower after the doors opened and instead of going back to my room I sat with the other guys while I ate breakfast.

They were both younger than me. One guy, Matt, had a funny-shaped head and was missing a few teeth. The other dude, Alan, looked like an ordinary twenty-something. Cute. Dark hair.

But kind of a badass. His mom dropped off a board game, Monopoly, for us. I watched them play. Alan ended up going directly to jail five turns in a row. I explained the concept of irony.

Twice a day they let us into the yard. It was a concrete pad with concrete walls and a chicken-wire ceiling. There were two soccer balls stuck in the corner, between the wall and ceiling, too high to reach. Sometimes I went out and sat on a bench.

On the way back to the pod, I asked the guard escorting us if the jail had a library. She took the others back and then led me down the hall to a broom closet. On a shelf behind the mops was a box of books. Everything I'd ever wanted to read but had never had the time for was in that box. Hemingway. Irving. I even found a paperback copy of Michael Crichton's *Travels*, a little-known memoir I'd tried forever to track down. I took a stack. I was crying. I don't know why. But I was crying. I felt cleaned out.

"Take that one, too," she said. The corrections officer was a motherish African-American woman. Pretty. Plump. She pointed at a Bible.

"Okay," I said.

"I don't know what your story is," she said. "But it will be okay. Do not let your heart be troubled. Read John 14."

"Okay."

"John 14. Don't forget."

Later that night, alone in my room, I did read it.

You may ask me for anything in my name, and I will do it.

Get me out of here, I prayed. *Please let me be with my family.*

The next morning, five days into a ten-day sentence, the man who delivered our breakfast had some news. "Renner," he said. "You're leaving today. Judge let you out early."

Julie was waiting in the lobby. She'd brought Casey and Lainey. I hugged them tight.

FIFTY-THREE

Beagle Strikes Back

Incarceration had taken a physical toll. I lost ten pounds in six days. Somewhere along the way I'd come into contact with some MRSA, too: because I left jail with an infection that rotted holes in my fingernails.

The ancillary effects of my arrest were unknown. I wasn't sure how bad it would get before the end. Wasn't even sure when the end would be. The biggest question was whether or not the media would cover my arraignment in Cuyahoga County Court, which was scheduled for June 19, my ninth wedding anniversary. Any decent press agent will tell you it's in your best interest to get ahead of the story, and so that's what I did. In a long post on Facebook, I talked about the arrest and my stay in jail.

The admission was immediately reposted on the Maura Murray Topix page.

The next day, Alden Olson, aka 112dirtbag, e-mailed the chair of the English Department at UAkron:

You might want to look into the fact that James W. Renner, an English instructor at the University of Akron, was recently jailed for contempt of court and later charged, as part of the same incident, with having assaulted a police officer at the Lakewood Municipal Court in Cuyahoga County.

I am the last person to discourage academic freedom, but Mr. Renner's overall conduct online, and to some degree in person, has troubled many who follow him. Some will wonder why the content of Renner's writings was not more carefully examined by the University of Akron before he was hired. To quote the UA website, "Safety is a top priority at UA, as evidenced by the wide variety of educational programs and safety services in place to help protect, inform and empower our students . . ."

Thank you very much.

Regards, Alden H. Olson

Hadley, MA

I play poker once a week with the chair of the English Department, and he's gotten to know me well. Still, friendship can go only so far. "If you really do end up with a felony, the university will have to fire you," he said. "There's nothing I can do."

The next hit came from Kevin Coughlin's camp, still stinging from my profile of the former gubernatorial candidate.

A Twitter account associated with the politician direct-tweeted it: "Disgraced liberal blogger James Renner to be arraigned tomorrow for felony assault of police officer."

It was only a matter of time before some newspaper jumped on the story. I could hear it, the sound of my reputation beginning to derail, a scenic-tour locomotive that took the last turn a bit too fast.

* * *

The day of my arraignment arrived. That's when you have to go in front of the judge and formally hear the charges read against you. Outside the courthouse, there were TV vans parked all along the road, antennas stretching into the summer air like the mini-skyscrapers of a temporary city. I was fucked.

But when I got to the courtroom, there were no cameras in sight. Turned out Ariel Castro was also in court that day, appearing for a pretrial a couple floors below me. Our cases were staggered such that every time I came to the courthouse, Castro was there, too. More of that fearful symmetry. Or maybe this time it was just a coincidence.

I was taken through a side door and reprocessed through the county's system, where felonies are prosecuted. Fingerprints. Mug shot. I spent the day in a dirty room with no windows, waiting for the bondsman to work out payment to the court. The place was filthy. Years of grime collected along the corners of the floor, slipping up the tilework like living depression. I watched guards in uniform escort prisoners down the hall. The county inmates were a different breed than the men I'd seen in muni jail. These men were beaten down, grizzled, worn. Through the whole ordeal, I was never so scared as I was those three hours in county lockup.

A short time later, Alden Olson reposted that scary video where he sits in his basement staring at the camera, laughing and leering, the one that ends with "Happy Anniversary." Except the day he reposted the video wasn't the anniversary of Maura's abduction—it was my daughter's first birthday. Then he posted a photograph of me beside a picture of Kenny from *South Park*. You know, the character who dies in every episode.

There were conference calls with a prosecutor and a police

captain in Massachusetts, but in the end the prosecutor would not go after Alden for stalking my family.

"What if, God forbid, he really does drive out here and attacks my wife or my daughter?" I asked the prosecutor.

He thought for a moment, then said, "Well, then we would have a pretty good case against him."

FIFTY-FOUR

The Fool

After the bondsman got me out, I took Julie to Greenhouse on East 4th for our anniversary. The kids were at her parents' for the night and it was just us again, the way we'd been in school, a couple out on a date. It seemed a little extravagant. Imprudent, even. Keeping me out of prison was not going to be cheap. We talked about Casey, our new concerns about how we were raising him. We talked about Lainey and how it felt like she was going to be easier. We talked about Julie's job, her plans for the next year. But eventually the conversation came around to Maura and what I was going to do with the book.

"I have to finish it," I said.

"Why?"

"I've already put so much time into it."

"I guess I just don't understand this one," she said. "Why her case? I get the Amy thing. She was your first crush, yada, yada. . . . But why Maura? Her family doesn't even want you to do it." She'd grown frustrated with the trips to New England, leaving her to parent two kids, and this was a long time coming. "Why can't you just find something else to write about?"

"Because it's the mystery of it. It's not like Amy. I'm not in love with Maura. I don't even think Maura was a good person. Nobody around her was a good person."

"So why do you want to explore that?"

"Because I know I'm smarter than whoever it was who planned all this. I can't quit. But I can promise you this will be the last one."

She shook her head, but smiled. "So finish it already, dumb-ass."

I went back to work.

In early August, we took the family to Ocean City, Maryland, and I met a psychic there I want to tell you about. Over the years, I'd heard from hundreds of psychics who wanted to talk about true crime cases. And in all that time, I'd met only one woman who convinced me she had the gift.

She was an old lady who lived on Cleveland's West Side. She worked closely with Amy Mihaljevic's family after her abduction. And though her help did not bring resolution, it produced evidence in the most unexpected way. After Amy's body was found in that wheat field in Ashland County, the psychic visited the scene and took a picture of the churned-up dirt where her body had been. When the Polaroid developed, a man's face could be seen in the shadows of the broken earth. It wasn't the impression of a face like you're thinking, like those pictures where you can see vases or faces if you look hard enough. No. This face was detailed. Ethereal, but defined. I saw it myself. The FBI were so freaked out about it, they had it analyzed by their forensics people. They determined that the film had not been manipulated.

There's a boardwalk in Ocean City that stretches for a mile, beginning at an amusement park by the pier. Along the way, you pass sizzling funnel cake stands and arcades full of twenty-year-old video games, and places where you can get henna tattoos. There's this authentic haunted house, too, from the sixties, the kind you ride, and it still makes you jump. Every hundred yards there's a street performer doing a jig beside an overturned hat. And gulls by the hundreds ride the breeze rolling out to the ocean, diving after dropped hot dogs.

Not far from the haunted house an alley snakes away from the boardwalk. I was holding Julie's hand, enjoying a late walk, and I looked that way in the dark and I saw her sign. PSYCHIC JEAN. And for some reason I was drawn by the romantic idea that I should visit her and ask about Maura. There was something about that night I'm not explaining well. A sense of freedom, of possibility. A feeling that all my troubles were petty and had been left far behind in Ohio, and that none of it really mattered. Or that nothing mattered more than we mattered to each other. I don't know. Maybe it was the ocean.

Jean invited us in. She was a carefully ancient woman, bent over a bit. She brought us into her apartment and motioned for Julie to sit on the couch by the TV, which was playing that scene from *Misery* where poor Sheldon gets hobbled.

"I'd like you to tell me what you can about a young woman who went missing a few years ago," I said.

Jean sighed. "You want me to find this girl? Tell you where she is?"

"Yes."

She nodded. "Okay. Let's do this." She walked over to a nook behind a cotton partition, motioned for me to follow. "But I can only tell you what I see." Julie started after us, but Jean put up a hand. "No, dear. You must not enter." I went in alone.

I sat across from the woman at a round table. She produced a stack of well-worn tarot cards.

"Cut the deck three times," she said.

I obliged.

"Put twenty-five dollars on top." Sure. There's a bottom line. Always. But hey, I knew psychics enough to know this was cheap. Weirdly cheap.

I gave her the money and the cards and she made the green disappear. She began to place the cards in a pattern upon the tablecloth: the Hermit, upside down; the Sun; a guy being stabbed by swords; and, on the very top of everything, the Fool.

She looked over the cards at me, and I was struck by the beauty of her eyes. Such an old face, full of hardship, but those eyes . . . Were they violet, even? I heard once that only Elizabeth Taylor had violet eyes.

"There is a lot of darkness here," she said. "You have traveled. But you have much traveling to do still."

"And what about her?" I asked. I hadn't come to hear about me.

"She was not traveling alone," said Jean, with confidence. I had told her nothing of Maura's case, or even her name, nothing more than she was a young woman who had gone missing. "Her car was left behind. And then she left with this other person. She wanted to be lost. You will not find her. She does not want to be found. Her life was sadness, bad luck. She wanted to escape this."

"Where did she go?"

"I cannot see her. She is either dead or the darkness is hiding her." Jean's eyes opened. They stared back at me, accusatory. "You went into her past."

"Yes."

"As far as her school years, didn't you?"

"Yes."

"Why? It's so much sadness."

I shrugged.

"You thought this would be an adventure. But her bad luck has rubbed off on you, hasn't it?"

I didn't say anything. I heard Julie stir on the couch in the other room.

"Why did you welcome this darkness? I need to ask you: Do you ever feel possessed?"

"By work."

Jean nodded. "Yes. You must leave this. Go. As quickly as you can. Leave it behind. Before the darkness follows you home."

She waved her arms over the cards as if to wash them off, and I took this as a sign to leave. I stood and thanked Jean for her time. The woman put a cold hand on my arm, staying me a moment.

"This young woman you're trying to find. She was her own . . ." Then she shook her head and went silent.

"What?"

"I don't want to say."

"She was her own *what*?"

"She was her own disaster."

FIFTY-FIVE

Everybody Lies

By the time I got around to writing the first lines of this book, I had filled a large box with information related to Maura's disappearance: court transcripts; interviews; photographs; newspapers; a copy of that book, *Not Without Peril*. The first thing I did was reread everything. Revisiting the e-mails people had written to me over the years opened up new avenues of investigation.

One of the things I rediscovered was this e-mail from a woman named Samantha, one of my Irregulars:

> *I am not sure if this is completely out there or not—
> but i was reading your post on the items found in Maura's
> car and noted her Stop and Shop card number. I was inter-
> ested in seeing if I could pull up a list of items purchased
> under that number. I went to the Stop and Shop website. I
> could enter the card number, which was associated with*

Maura's name, but it requested I register an online account to view any information. I did not feel comfortable doing that. However, the site automatically filled in fields for the registration form—I'm assuming based off of what Maura provided when she set up the account. It included the phone number and address for Fred's house in Weymouth—and the email address: aasic@aol.com

After a google search—that email address seemed to be associated with a Richard Thousand, living in Cleveland OH. He commented on a few guest books using that address, one of which listed his location as Cleveland. A facebook page for Richard Thousand in Cleveland OH shows hes a registered nurse, and was in college around Maura's time (class of 2003).

Could be nothing. Typo on the email address or maybe she gave a fake one to avoid spam—but I thought it was at least interesting.

I found that Facebook page for Richard Thousand and sent him an e-mail, asking about the strange way Maura's shopping card linked back to one of his old e-mail accounts. I noted that his profile showed a photograph of a dog instead of his face. A search of Google didn't find any photographs of him, either. That's odd in this hyper-social-media era. But not *that* odd. He got back to me immediately.

Very Interesting! I did attend a meeting at U Mass shortly after graduating from Nursing School in 2003. I was there for approximately a week and signed for a card at the Stop and Shop close to where I was staying because

they had some money off on gas. Of course, while there I talked to several nurses attending the University and I do remember talking quite some time with a girl who fits Maura's profile from your website. We were both runners and I grew up in Upstate New York and camped and hiked many of the same areas that she had in New Hampshire. I remember her mentioning a boyfriend in Oklahoma because I had told her I had moved to Ohio from Kansas and she said she was planning on getting a job there. She asked me about the kind of area it was. I also had been in the Air Force and she mentioned some military training, but I don't remember her mentioning West Point Academy— but that was a while ago. As for the card, I don't think she would have stolen it from me since I keep a very keen eye on my wallet and only carry the bare minimum. I am notorious about dumping these cards anywhere because they aren't credit cards and we don't have these stores in Ohio so I could have left it anywhere on campus. I still do this since I travel a lot but I guess I will be more careful in the future. I was rather shocked by what I read about her disappearance but I had a co worker in Kansas disappear and there were a lot of strange theories but they eventually found out that BTK was her neighbor and actually abducted her from her home and killed her.

Hmm. Now, according to my own litmus test, Richard Thousand had just made himself an outlier. Here was a man tangentially connected to two national mysteries: the BTK murders and Maura's disappearance. He had my attention, but his story seemed plausible, given Maura's history of petty larceny. So, yeah, I could see her stealing this man's shopping card for the twenty cents she might save on gas.

I posted Thousand's story on my blog, and it blew up like I thought it might. Who was this guy? Everyone wanted to know. One anonymous commenter summed it up nicely:

"Thousand knows TWO people who disappeared (as an earlier poster mentioned), and one was killed by the BTK? His entire account is an odd mix of facile, hinky and 'look at me' dramatic. Look into this weirdo."

Thousand was reading, too. He got back to me quickly.

I have to apologize to Maura and you and set the record straight. About two years ago I came across the story of Maura's disappearance and due to many commonalities between us I got hooked into the investigation. I came across the photos and saw the card with the number on the back. One night I attempted to access the card to see if there was anything interesting to the investigation. I don't even remember the specifics but when I provided my e mail address it gave me access to the card account. Afterward I got worried about doing this and dropped my interest in her case. When I got your e mail I got spooked and sent an e mail that gave the impression she found my card. While checking out your blog last night I came across the item about the card and was shocked that my e mail was there and people discussing that she stole my card and then changed the information on it. This is a tragic situation for both Maura and her family and I don't want to do anything to perpetuate the idea that she was a thief or untrustworthy. Further-

more, I didn't write the email for attention and I have an
alibi for my whereabouts on the night she disappeared so
your readers can relax. I still wish you well with your book.
	Rick

So did he even meet Maura while at UMass? I asked him in a follow-up e-mail.

> *I was in u mass looking into the master program in*
> *2003 and talked to some nurses. That is one reason I got*
> *drawn into this story. Everything in the e mail was true*
> *except talking to a particular student that had a boyfriend*
> *in Oklahoma. If I met her I think I would have remem-*
> *bered that name so I would say no. FYI. Marine Hedges*
> *worked for years in our hospital coffee shop in Wichita*
> *Kansas. I knew her only because she made me food every*
> *Thursday, otherwise I had no real connection to her, Why*
> *I brought that up was that prior to finding out that it was*
> *BTK, there were many theories some bordering on the bi-*
> *zarre about what happened to her. Everyone was totally*
> *shocked when they learned the truth that she was just un-*
> *lucky that night.*

It took a lot to give me the willies, but everything about this exchange with Thousand disturbed me. I didn't know what to make of it, really. I sent the info to the Cold Case Unit in New Hampshire, and they were interested enough to ask me a couple of questions about my contact with him. But, as far as I know, noth- ing more ever came of it, and I have yet to find any direct link be- tween Maura and Rick Thousand. And, after all, BTK confessed to killing Hedges. He admitted to waiting for her inside her house before strangling her and posing her body for pictures outside his church before returning to a Boy Scout campout.

As Psychic Jean would say, maybe Thousand just brought some of that darkness back to Cleveland with him. No one would notice a little more darkness in our city.

FIFTY-SIX

Billy, Don't Lose My Number

One day, not too long after my arrest, Billy Rausch called me on my cell phone. This was the first time I'd spoken to him. He had ignored my e-mails and phone messages for years.

"Thank you for calling me, Billy," I said.

"It's Bill," he replied. "*Bill.* Don't call me Billy."

He had called to ask me to delete a photograph I had posted on the blog. His wife appeared in the picture and he didn't want her to be identifiable to any of the weirdos who browsed my articles.

"I'll delete it today," I said.

"Good. Thank you."

"I have so many questions, Bill. Can you please just talk to me for a few minutes?"

He sighed. "Yeah. All right. Go ahead."

"How did you and Maura meet?"

Bill laughed. It was an ironic laugh. "She got an honor code violation at West Point," he said. "She stole a granola bar from a store. There were other problems, too. Anyway, that's how I met her." At the time, Bill served as a cadet liaison to the West Point adjudicators, though he never worked on Maura's case. He was struck by her beauty, regardless of her troubles. They started dating.

He wanted to clear up a couple of points, now that we were talking. He said that Fred never tried to keep him from talking to me and, as far as he knows, never told Maura's friends to keep quiet, either. Whatever else happened that last weekend, Fred was definitely helping Maura find a new car, he explained, adding that they had visited the same dealership where he had purchased his own car.

Bill also said that the party Maura had gone to the night she crashed Fred's car was held off-campus, even though Kate had told me, on more than one occasion, that it was held in Sara's dorm room.

One more thing. That e-mail that was on top of Maura's boxes? Bill confirmed that it had to do with him seeing another woman but that it was a bit more complicated than the police let on. "The e-mail was about a girl I was dating at the time I met Maura," he said. "We had broken up, Maura and I. And I saw this other woman again. We were broken up at the time, though."

Bill said he didn't know about Maura's affair with her track coach and that she had never spoken about running away. Then again, Maura never told him about her pending fraud charges, either. "Clearly, I didn't know her as well as I thought I did."

Later, Bill shared some more stories, in a series of e-mails. "I'm trusting you with these memories and hope that you can put them to good use," he wrote.

When he was in high school, Bill ran cross-country and track, but it wasn't a passion. For Maura, it clearly was. "Her time running was special for her—a sacred time. She also loved a good cup of coffee and so did I. We enjoyed seeking out local coffee shops when we were together and spent a lot of time reading and talking over coffee in any unique shop we could find." She would often return from her runs with two hot coffees in hand, one for her and one for Bill. "It was the kind of selfless act she would often do."

He told me another story about a time she visited Ohio to help with the wedding of one of Bill's family members. There was a last-minute venue change and Maura stayed up all night, helping decorate the new space. "We both believed in the power of good will and she regularly tutored other students who were less gifted and was very good at explaining complex issues in a very simple and effective way."

I could tell that Bill was hurting. When I spoke to him, there was a resignation in his voice that sounded hollow and worn. In the span of a few years he had lost his girlfriend and his sister. He'd served in Iraq. And somehow he'd come out the other side and built a new family. I understood now why he wanted to distance himself from all this.

"It's not my place, and you've dealt with more than I have," I told him. "You have someone you can talk to?"

His sigh was audible. "Yes. I do. Thanks for your concern." We left it at that.

FIFTY-SEVEN

Closure Is for Doors

I do these library gigs. I stand in front of a roomful of people and talk about true crimes or tell scary stories for an hour and they pay me $200. I have a PowerPoint about the Lisa Pruett murder, complete with autopsy photographs. Usually, though, they want me to talk about Amy Mihaljevic, and that's what I did one night at the Grafton Public Library, a forty-minute drive west of Cleveland.

I read from the first chapter of my book on Amy's case, which begins: *I fell in love with Amy Mihaljevic not long before her body was discovered lying facedown in an Ashland County wheat field.* I'd given this talk about fifty times before, but something felt different that night. Maybe it was the fact that the room was filled to capacity for once. I found a little extra oomph, a bit more bang-pow. It was going so well, I decided to tell a story about the case that I'd never shared in public before.

"I want to tell you about what happened to me in Key West,"

I began. Amy's photo, that one with the side-saddle ponytail, was projected on the wall behind me.

This was in 2008, and a retired FBI agent had just told me he believed that Dean Runkle, a former middle school teacher, was the best suspect the police had ever found. Runkle was a science teacher in Amherst; that's Amherst, Ohio, not Massachusetts. He kept a menagerie in his classroom, terrariums of snakes and large tanks full of tropical fish. He kept a human skeleton in his closet that he said was a young girl he'd disliked. The FBI had discovered love letters he'd written to a former middle school student. I was told by the principal that Runkle was investigated, twice, for relationships with his prepubescent students. Oh, and a witness to Amy's abduction picked Runkle's photograph out of a lineup of thirty men. At the time of Amy's murder, he lived a mile away from where her body was found in rural Ashland County, and, according to a dozen former students, he volunteered at the nature center in Bay Village, where Amy had written her name and phone number on a ledger inside.

I was compelled to speak to this man.

By the time I got his name, Runkle had quit teaching. His principal told me that when asked to provide fingerprints to renew his license, he'd refused and resigned. He disappeared for a spell and then resurfaced in a Key West homeless shelter, where he lived for several months.

On my own dime, I flew down to the Keys and stayed a couple nights at a hotel not far from Hemingway's old place. I didn't know where Runkle lived. I showed his photograph around town and got some solid leads at first—some remembered him as the old man who played ragtime piano at local bars (Runkle, I knew, had played ragtime piano at Disneyland). Eventually, I discovered he was managing the Wendy's on the northern side of the island. But he'd called in sick that day, and nobody knew exactly where he lived.

I had only a half hour left before I had to leave the island in order to catch my departing flight out of Miami. Despondent, I found myself at a stop sign on the northeast quadrant of the island. It had been some time since I'd prayed, possibly many years. But at that moment, I called out to God or the universe or Amy. Whoever was listening. "Help me find this man."

At that moment, Dean Runkle walked in front of my car.

I have educated friends who are atheists. I wish I had the luxury of doubt. And I did doubt—until that moment. Never again.

I got out. We spoke. He didn't admit anything. But he said there were things in his life he couldn't remember.

I took his picture, and then I left.

When I finished telling my story, a woman came up to me and gave me a hug. I stayed and signed books for a bit. And that's when I noticed the man in the back of the room. He looked oddly familiar. It was Mark Mihaljevic, Amy's father.

I ended up at his house that night and he microwaved me a hamburger. We sat at his kitchen table and ate burgers and talked about a lot of things, but not about his daughter. There is a happier parallel universe, I am fairly certain, in which this man is my father-in-law.

I sat with my sister Barb at the back of Judge Daniel Gaul's courtroom and watched as a man was sent to prison. The Lakewood police had helped my sister with her stalker situation and told the dogcatcher to never go near her again. But he was never charged. She's less trusting now, and that's sad. Still, it could have been worse.

My lawyer escorted me to the desk in front of the judge. Gaul was a skinny fellow in a black robe, and his eyes had this amused look. I think he was amused by me.

"What in the world happened?" he asked.

I told him my story, such as it was. I shrugged. "It all happened in the span of thirty seconds. I can't explain why I acted the way I did."

"I looked at your history. You also have, what, eleven tickets, speeding tickets? That to me suggests manic episodes. You seeing a psychologist?"

"Yes."

"On medication?"

"Yes."

Judge Gaul nodded. "You have to stop this. This behavior. Eventually you're going to knock on someone's door or anger the wrong man and you're going to get yourself killed. You know that, right? You keep this up and someone will pull a gun on you and kill you."

"I know."

"So stop."

"Yes, sir."

The felony assault charge didn't stick. The witness from the hallway who saw the cop throw me against the wall signed an affidavit stating that the police officer was the one who instigated the fight. The courtroom video backed us up, too. I ended up pleading to a misdemeanor charge of "Attempted Resisting Arrest," whatever that means. The judge waived all fines and sentenced me to six months probation.

Later that day, Ariel Castro wrapped a bedsheet around his neck and committed suicide in his cell.

*   *   *

I had a book signing in Bedford, I was at a booth in the city square, and the signing was part of the city's annual elf festival. A man came by and we struck up a conversation. Turned out he was a retired ranger for the Metroparks. I decided to tell him about the time I was nearly abducted from the woods on Memphis, by the kiddie park. His eyes grew wide. I could tell I had upset him.

"You ever looked into the former director of the Metroparks?" he asked me.

"For what?"

"Just do yourself a favor and check it out."

I did. When I got home I pulled him up on Google. The former director's name was Vern Hartenburg. Soon as I saw his picture, I knew. This was *my* boogeyman. The guy from the park that day, who had chased me into the woods and down the railroad tracks. Hartenburg had been arrested for exposing himself in the Metroparks. To be specific, he was arrested at the park on Memphis Avenue. The *same* small park where he'd chased after me in 1991.

The Metroparks are publicly funded. As such, they are subject to public records requests. I pulled Hartenburg's personnel file, not sure what I was looking for. Did I expect to find a handwritten note? *Hey, I just want to let you guys know that I once tried to snatch a kid in the park.*

Turned out Hartenburg suffered a nervous breakdown and checked himself into a psych ward years ago. He had to request a leave of absence from the Metroparks and some of the details came out then. Funny thing: Hartenburg's breakdown occurred ten days after Amy Mihaljevic's abduction, in 1989.

I had to meet this man.

I found Hartenburg in the gated community of Lakeside, on the shores of Lake Erie. It's a Christian commune of sorts, and he was working as a general landscaper for the place while his wife was away on a pilgrimage to the Holy Land. He rode over to my van in a golf cart and we talked through the window.

I told him I recognized him as the man who had tried to snatch me away from the Metroparks, in Old Brooklyn. He shook his head. Said he didn't know anything about it. Then he told me a story about how he was sexually assaulted as a kid and how he had been raped for years. It was that abuse that compelled him to act out later, he explained. "I'm sorry for what I've done."

I asked him why, of all the moments in his life, he decided to have himself committed to a mental hospital just days after Amy Mihaljevic was abducted. That was a hell of a coincidence, I said.

Hartenburg shrugged. "It was just when all that abuse caught up with me," he said.

I drove away, more confused than ever.

Only one man abducted Amy, and yet there were so many likely suspects in the case. What did that say about the world? What sense does any of it make?

FIFTY-EIGHT

Failed Tests

At the start of every year, my wife's school offers enrichment programs for teachers, short presentations in the multipurpose room that are meant to pep everyone up for the new semester. Sometimes the speakers test the teachers with logic puzzles or riddles as a way to improve their attention skills. In the fall of 2013, one of the presenters posed a riddle meant to identify potential psychopaths. It was a funny exercise. Or meant to be.

Julie came home at the end of the day, wanting to share. She was curious to see how quickly I would solve it. Or maybe to see if I could solve it at all.

Here's the gist: A single man attends his mother's funeral. During the wake, he meets a fantastic young woman and falls madly in love. But he forgets her name and nobody he talks to afterward can identify her. How does he track her down?

"He kills his father," I said, without missing a beat. "She'll probably come to his funeral, too."

Julie's expression changed from jovial to shocked. "Jesus," she said. "I thought you'd figure it out. But . . . but that was so quick. That's how your mind works? I mean, that didn't even enter my mind. At all. You got it right away."

"Sorry," I said.

She shivered.

When I finished the first draft of this book, I found some holes in my reporting that needed filling. I'd never gotten much on Butch Atwood, the guy who'd last spoken to Maura Murray on Wild Ammonoosuc Road. After some digging, I tracked down his widow. She was living in Florida.

Her name is Barbara. She married Butch in 1993 and they lived together in the house near the crash site with his mother, Violet. He may have been a big, scary-looking man, but he was a soft mark, she said. Butch cried when their springer spaniel died. He liked to hunt, fish, and ride his motorcycle when the weather was clear.

Their lives changed forever the night Maura wrecked her car.

"He asked Maura if she was okay," she explained. "He offered to call the police to help her with the car. She asked him not to. 'No, no, no,' she said. He came inside then and told us that there was an accident. We called 911 anyway, and Butch went outside to finish paperwork in his bus. By the time the cops got there, she was gone."

Butch went out driving later to try to locate Maura, but he never found another sign of her.

When the case became national news, the police asked Butch to take a lie detector test. He flunked it, Barbara said. And the cop in the room told him it was time for him to come clean. "But there was a lot of things wrong with Butch that made the results unreliable. He had high blood pressure, diabetes, AF, COPD, and he was obese. So they gave him another test, which he passed."

Barbara does not believe that Butch had anything to do with Maura's disappearance. She said that Butch figured Maura was meeting someone up there and it was that person who picked her up. It was the only explanation for how she could vanish so quickly.

In March of 2009, Barbara went to take care of her sister in Massachusetts. While she was gone, Butch caught the flu. He couldn't breathe. Doctors discovered that the arteries feeding his heart were blocked. They put in a stent, did three bypass surgeries. Shortly after returning home, Butch complained of stomach pain. He went back in. The doctors opened him up. His guts were full of cancer. They took out most of his upper intestine. Eventually they released him. Butch was home a week and a day before he died.

I needed to know more about Maura's classmates at UMass, too. At the time she disappeared, Maura was completing her clinicals, a major requirement for her nursing degree. Clinicals are a way for students to gain firsthand experience in nursing before graduation. It's the hardest part of the program, the moment where students finally find out if they can cut it or not. Maura was in a class of seventy, which was divided into smaller groups of six to eight. Bonds formed quickly. On top of this, Maura's course load that last semester was brutal. She was taking classes in pharmacology, mental health, and maternity in addition to a research class.

With a little help from my Irregulars, I discovered the names of the other students in Maura's clinical group: Christina Linscott, Noelle Lepore, Brian McKaskell, Patricia Johnson, and Martha Nagle. Maura carpooled with these students during her rotations, two days a week. They divided their time between Norwood Hospital's labor and delivery unit and the Providence Behavioral

Health Hospital in Holyoke, reporting to staff at 7 A.M. They were assigned patients and worked until 2 P.M. Then, they would carpool back to UMass. Classmates described Maura as "very quiet, reserved."

After Maura disappeared, a detective came to speak to them, asking what they knew about her character. But there wasn't much they could offer police. It wasn't like Maura wanted to hang out after clinicals or anything.

Of course, I found an extra layer of weirdness while researching Maura's clinicals. Everything about this case is odd. It's always hard to know what is a clue and what is just another bizarre coincidence. Here's what happened.

When I contacted Martha Nagle via Facebook I got this message back:

> I'd like to help but I'm also related to Maura and I don't feel comfortable talking about this with you. Only out of respect for Maura's family. Thank you anyway. Good luck with your research.

That's a red flag.

How, exactly, was Martha related to Maura? Martha was Asian-American, so it wasn't by blood. A quick look at her background showed that she'd gone by many other names: Martha Park; Martha Vivar. I asked her to help me fill in the blanks. She told me that she was related by marriage.

I noted that at one time Martha had had connections to the tiny town of Taunton, Mass. As you may recall, Taunton was the neighborhood where someone called "Observer" had written on a Maura Murray message board in support of the theory that Maura was now living in Canada. I went back and reread the original

GeoCities post. I noticed something unusual in the wording that I'd missed up till now. Here's the pertinent section:

> *Sometime between 12 MN and 1 AM Maura driving her Saturn struck and critically injured the UMass student Petrit Vasi leaving him for dead.*

That "12 MN" bit suddenly stuck out. I don't know anyone who refers to midnight that way; I'm used to seeing "12 A.M." But you know who does write it that way? Nurses. "12 MN" is medical dictation they teach to nursing students so that midnight is never mixed up with noon on patient charts.

I asked Martha if she was the author of that post.

Fuck you. How's that for comment? she wrote.

It got me thinking about Canada again. Could Maura really be hiding in Quebec?

Can someone really disappear in this day and age?

FIFTY-NINE

How to Disappear

As a matter of fact, people do it all the time.

One of my favorite unsolved mysteries is the story of Joseph Newton Chandler. Chandler was an electrical engineer for a Cleveland chemical manufacturer. He put in twelve years before he was laid off in 1997. He kept in contact with a couple of people from work after that and lived in a studio on the East Side of town. Then in 2002, he ate a bullet in his bathroom.

Police used his birth certificate to track down next of kin. And that's where things got weird. See, when they got Joe Chandler's sister on the horn, she was quite surprised—her brother had died in a traffic accident in 1945. The guy who'd committed suicide in Cleveland had stolen her brother's social security number in 1978 and had been living under an assumed name for twenty-four years. He left $82,000 in a bank account and, as best as detectives can figure, committed suicide because he'd been diagnosed with cancer.

Internet sleuths have suggested "Joe Chandler" was actually the Zodiac Killer. Some believe he was Jim Morrison (no joke). But the most likely true identity of Joe Chandler, in my opinion, is a guy named Stephen Campbell, who was an electrical engineer from Cheyenne, Wyoming, who tried to kill his wife's lover with a homemade bomb. Campbell disappeared in 1982.

Some people, even people in very public positions, just want to disappear and start over someplace new. Olivia Newton-John's boyfriend faked his own death in 2005 and was found living in Mexico five years later. Mystery matriarch Agatha Christie disappeared for ten days in 1926, in what many have proposed was an attempt to frame her cheating husband for her murder.

It's a common fantasy, right? The idea that we might simply walk away from this life and live as someone new in some faraway place.

But it's getting harder to pull off. With the Internet and all its various methods of invading privacy, it has gotten easier to track people down. Olivia Newton-John's boyfriend was found by tracking an IP address that was monitoring one of the sites devoted to his disappearance.

It's harder. But not impossible, given the proper motivation.

Some shelters and organizations for abused women have networks of well-placed contacts who help clients set up new identities to escape abusers. It's an underground railroad that rivals the federal government's witness protection program. In some instances, these contacts help women change their names, social security numbers, job history. Here's the mission statement for the House of Ruth: *The House of Ruth Maryland leads the fight to end violence against women and their children by confronting the attitudes, behaviors and systems that perpetuate it, and by providing victims with the services necessary to rebuild their lives safely and free of fear.*

During the course of my research I was contacted by a social worker in a southern state who had read a post I'd written about the House of Ruth. She read through the rest of the blog, delving deep into the mystery of Maura's disappearance, and came to believe it was possible that Maura had used this system to start a new life. My source said she was one of the "well-placed contacts" called on to hide victims of abuse. Sometimes she would get a call in the middle of the night and have to immediately drive to a location to pick up an abused woman. She would then help the woman disappear.

"Not all of what they do is 100% legal," she wrote to me in a Facebook message after I verified her employment. "It's a huge network of people worldwide that assist with whatever is needed when called upon. I can attest that these organizations are very good at what they do. This is a surefire way to disappear with little to no resources and no street sense, neither of which Maura seemed to possess."

She believes Maura may have fooled one of these organizations in order to escape her legal troubles, something that this woman takes as a personal insult. But if that's what she did, she could be very well hidden.

"You have a better chance of finding the Holy Grail," the social worker wrote. "Tight-lipped is an understatement. People involved with these types of organizations have a lot to lose and keep better secrets than the Pentagon. I don't know how you could explore this further but certain things are leading me to believe this is a really viable theory."

But how could someone like Maura get by without using her social security number?

"Hypothetical: I let them 'borrow' mine. Good credit history, clean background, etc. Then, when they're where they're going, a new identity is set up and mine is returned to me. It really is like an underground railroad. And I would happily serve time in jail before giving anyone up. I would go to drastic measures to protect them."

The idea of Maura "borrowing" someone's social security number is intriguing. When my private investigator friend ran Maura's background, he discovered that another social security number was somehow connected to her identity for a short time. It linked back to a woman named Lori, who still lived in Hanson, a few streets from where Maura grew up. I could never find a direct connection between Lori and Maura, but Maura does have a history of using someone else's name and identity—at least to steal food. I wonder....

SIXTY

Oh, Canada!

Several people believe they have come face-to-face with Maura Murray in the years since the accident on Wild Ammonoosuc Road. According to reports from the *Whitman-Hanson Express,* Maura was spotted in Barton, Vermont, in 2005. A young woman who looked like Maura attended a church service in town. She called herself "Raykel," and abruptly left when the minister starting talking about Father's Day. A year later a woman in the company of an older man mouthed the words "Help me" to a witness at a Cumberland Farms store in Hillsborough, New Hampshire. The witness thought it could have been Maura.

A cashier who worked at Butson's grocery store in Woodsville believed she sold liquor to Maura less than an hour before her accident on Wild Ammonoosuc Road. She said Maura was with two other women, and one had dark hair just like Maura. She looked at their IDs. Two were from Massachusetts; one was from either New York or Connecticut. After she heard that Maura was missing, the woman reported the sighting to her supervisor. When Fred Murray heard about it, he caused a scene at the store, demanding the videotape before the police could see it. But Butson's didn't have surveillance. Strangely, the Murray family kept this sighting a secret until the woman contacted me in 2014 and they were forced to acknowledge the tip.

More recent credible sightings have come out of Quebec, Canada. There's that infamous GeoCities post, of course. And there are two more.

On April 8, 2009, "Tourist in Canada" posted the following message on the Amherst, Massachusetts, Topix page from a computer in Brockton: "I saw Maura Murray alive and well in Sherbrooke, Quebec. I approached her and said 'Hi Maura.' She turned toward me and said 'Hi,' then gasped and looked like she was going to pass out from shock. I have no doubt this was Maura Murray. She is apparently alive and well and living in Canada. When I saw her she was with a very handsome young man."

The same day, someone from the Houston, Texas, region posted a similar message on the Topix page from St-Étienne-de-Beauharnois, a small town outside Montreal. "Maura Murray was seen in Quebec City, Quebec Province. She is alive and well. Very well. Her new squeeze is a hunk."

Around Thanksgiving, 2013, I got a call from Lance Reenstierna, the guy from Boston who had helped me preserve Alden Olson's threatening YouTube videos. He had gotten "consumed" by Maura's mystery and had taken some time off to work on other things so that his interest in the case didn't become a full-blown obsession. But, he said, "I'm getting back into it. I've decided to make a documentary. Can I fly you out to Boston?"

Sure I could do Boston, I told him. Or, we could go on an adventure and actually try to find her. I filled him in on the Canadian sightings.

"Okay," he said. "Let's do it."

In early December, I hopped a flight from Akron to Boston Logan. Lance, who has more than a passing resemblance to Peter Sarsgaard, picked me up and we drove north. Along for the adventure were two of his friends: Tim Pilleri and Josh Leonard. They'd worked together on various projects over the years and had once written and produced a popular mystery-dinner theater program together.

We were briefly detained at the border. Lance told the guy who checked our passports that we were on a pilgrimage to a famous Montreal church. I was convinced that my misdemeanor had pinged the guard's computer and we would be spending the night in some secret Homeland Security jail. But the border agents were just curious about four dudes entering their country with a van full of camera equipment. After they thoroughly checked the vehicle, and confiscated a staple gun I had brought along to hang MISSING posters, they let us cross.

We drove to Sherbrooke first. It's a college town with a brick-and-mortar center at the confluence of two major rivers, once home to the Mohawk and Abenaki tribes before it was pillaged by French Canadians. It reminded me of a mid-sized Pennsylvania city, something like State College or Wilkes-Barre, a quaint downtown with suburban sprawl surrounding it like slow cancer.

Sherbrooke is French-speaking, but the residents are kinder to Americans than the Québécois of Montreal (you can still find English menus here). None of us spoke a lick of French, and I found it disconcerting to wander around a town where I could not read signs or advertisements. I felt illiterate.

We fanned out around the downtown area, taping Maura's MISSING posters to streetlamps and storefront windows. I went inside every bar, Tim surreptitiously capturing my interviews on his flip cam. I spoke in slow English to the proprietors. We didn't get our first decent lead until I showed Maura's photograph to the barista at La Brûlerie on rue Wellington. "Yes," the young woman said, studying the picture. "I believe I've seen this woman. I think she came in here before."

On the other side of town later that night, we were canvassing rue Therrien outside Bar Studio Sex, a darkly lit strip club, and I showed Maura's picture to a man loitering outside.

"I know her," he said.

"This woman?" I asked. "Where is she?"

"She's in the morgue," he said, and walked away. I jogged after him.

"You really know this woman?"

"Yes. I knew her. Couple years ago. She OD'd, man. I'm American, you know. I came here because I was being spied on. The government, man. They're after me."

This man was not sane, I quickly realized. Or maybe he was tweaking. Whatever was going on with him, he was far from a credible witness. He told me a little more about his conspiracy theories and then continued down the road, talking to himself.

The next morning, we stopped at a fitness center called Maxi Club, located behind our hotel. When I showed the manager Maura's photo, she didn't hesitate. "This woman came in three weeks ago," she said. "But I haven't seen her since."

We drove to St-Étienne-de-Beauharnois then, discovered it was little more than an intersection with a candy store, and returned to Sherbrooke for the night. Although we were getting leads there, we felt it was in our best interest to visit Quebec City before returning home the following day.

Fuck, Quebec City is cold. Like brutally cold. Arctic Circle cold. It's so far north of Akron that the sun sets an hour and ten minutes earlier there. It is home to half a million Canucks.

Quebec was once "Kebec," an Indian word meaning "where the river narrows," fitting because the St. Lawrence River squeezes around the city before emptying into the Atlantic. Tall fort ramparts still surround the oldest quarter, Vieux Québec. Driving through downtown, one sees a strange mishmash of European and American architecture that becomes decidedly more tacky the farther your drive downhill.

We visited grocery stores and gas stations and bars. Our group became separated at one point, and during that time Tim and I happened upon a hipstery section of the city, full of pubs and narrow shops along St-Joseph Est. There was a vintage album store there called Le Knock-Out and I left a couple flyers with the woman behind the counter. She was a total punk and seemed quite curious about who we were and why we were so interested in this missing woman, but her English was very broken and it was hard to understand half of what she was saying.

A week later, I got an e-mail from her.

> *2 of us maybe saw Maura Murray in Quebec on monday december 2 and saturday december 7. We speak with a girl who looks like the one you're looking for. The similitude with pictures are soooo intense. And her speach was weird . . . I think you have my phone number.*
>
> *Roxann*

I wrote back right away, and she gave me a little more:

> *Just let you know that the girl we have seen here in QC look like the pictures of Maura Murray but older of course! She looks like around 34 . . . Like I said in another email. It's someone who looks like the girl but older. That's it. And I do not look for something back or visibility or anything like that. I don't care about that. I just wanted to do my citizen job. The girl here was muchhhhhh look like the picture but older. Just that.*
>
> *One of my friend was with me on that monday. He speachs english: he speaks with that girl. She was on bicycle (bike) in snow. sportive girl.*
>
> *I did not want to communicate with you at that time because you did not identify. But i talk with the police. He talked with NH police and i thought you too because the police told me you gave him my number phone.*
>
> *In fact, she asked for live music on monday here in Quebec. We (friend and I) told her that here, in qc, there is nothing on monday and tell her for thursay ou friday. She said she will not be there . . . she really want it MONDAY. And on saturday, i see her in bike on another street. Alone, in the snow with her bike. I notice it because she told us she would not be there and that clash me.*
>
> *She is REALLY look like the picture. We both (friend and I) have a great visual memory. She enters the record store slowly, watching. She was discreet. We wanted to give her a map with the name of venue of artist and she refused telling she was ok. She told us that here, in QC, people do not know their town, not like another places (that supposed she travels). She speaks at "I" and not*

"WE". She has a suit for winter, but cheap one, not a big "sportive." One colour suit. I know a lottt of people here so that I notice her on the street the saturday. She did not have make up.

She was really in good shape. No fat at all. Building athletic.

She stay around 15 minutes in the shop talking (english). She acts a little weird. She had a little "backpack" (dont know the word). My friend talk about music and how the city was "made" (streets) . . . She did not wanted to go to big show. Just some little.

You have some pictures on the net that are SOOOOO similar. I would never have contact police or you if my friend and I do not have a big suspicious. Hope it can help.

Bye bye.

:)

Was it possible that we had crossed paths with Maura Murray in Canada?

SIXTY-ONE

Poker Face

It was the pediatrician who finally figured out my son. This was halfway through Casey's second year at the bad kids' school. A kiddie psychiatrist had put him on meds, something called clonidine. The drugs had helped a little. He was less violent at home. But they made him so tired. And he was still being sent to that scary room with the padded walls most days. Out of an abundance of caution, we returned to his pediatrician. He's an older man with a practiced manner, one of those adults who speaks to kids with respect. He wrote us a prescription for a drug called Intuniv. "This is what I've been giving kids for thirty years," he said.

A lot of writers, when searching for a deus ex machina to get their characters out of a precarious situation near the end of a story, will resort to a drug. A magic pill, perhaps, to help the protagonist along. *Eat this to make you small.* . . . But sometimes that's how it is in real life, too.

Casey simply stopped having bad days. He stopped hitting

his teachers, stopped going to the "support" room. And while it's still too early to tell if we've come through the dark tunnel, it's a hell of a start.

"Take me with you the next time you go to the mountains to find that woman," he said to me recently. "I'll help you find her."

There's a young man in a photograph with Maura that was posted on the family's Web site. It was taken at a restaurant not long before she disappeared. The man is handsome and exotic. He looks slightly Asian. He is sitting beside Maura and they're smiling. They seem to be enjoying each other's company.

His name is David Whalen. I wanted to talk to him, just to get more background stories about Maura, but when I went to track him down, I couldn't find a Facebook page or an e-mail address or, really, anything other than his current ranking in the professional poker circuit. Over the last few years, David has made over $100,000 playing cards. Some of this is online poker, so it's hard to tell exactly how much he's banked. But it's a lot. He's good. And he keeps a very low profile.

I posted his picture on my blog and asked him to contact me for an interview. I didn't get any bites for months. And then I heard from a man named Sean, another high-stakes poker player, who often sat across from David at high-stakes tables.

Admittedly I am not very well versed in the case overall but I saw a quick blip related to the "Londonderry Ping," which I believe may have been the last outbound call to Maura's phone. The first thing that jumped out to me about that particular region is the proximity to both the Rockingham Park and the Seabrook Race track. These places stand out to me due to them being places where one can find poker games. It's relatively common for people who are regulars at Foxwoods (particularly those living in Central/Northeastern Mass.) to call in ahead and see what games are running at Foxwoods—if it's not busy and game selection is poor some people would just opt to head up to Seabrook or Salem and play lower money games in exchange for saving time/gas driving to Foxwoods.

I called Sean immediately. "Where is David now?" I asked.

"Last I heard, he was living in Canada. Gambling tax laws are better up there and you can still get away with playing online. There are some good tables in and around Montreal. But I heard he was living outside the city."

"Where?"

"Sherbrooke."

We went on the hunt, my Irregulars and I. A lawyer named Sam, who runs another site devoted to Maura's case, NotWithoutPeril, found David's Twitter account. He was using the handle David Tadas, a shortening of his middle name. Combing through his tweets, I discovered some alarming messages:

> *Well, if voluntary manslaughter is a crime, then yeah, I guess I'm a criminal.*

> *Oh, I get it, misread one girl for having a rape fantasy and all of a sudden I'm a "rapist."*

> *If I ever get charged with murder, I'll probably use the classic, "I Was Playing Simon Says," defense.*

Holy shit, right?

I posted some of the tweets on my blog. Later that day, David sent me an e-mail, using a temporary account linked to an IP address that tracked back to a computer in Connecticut.

"I have noticed that you continue to post about me on your website," he wrote. "It seems that you came across a picture of me in college and built a narrative about my potential involvement with Maura. Reading the posts/comments from strangers that speculate about my life based on ONE photo makes me nauseous. I was a friend of Maura's in high school/college. We weren't particularly close, but we did share some friends in common. This is the beginning and end of any useful information I can provide. I have a weird, silly, and yes, sometimes dark sense of humor. It horrifies me that someone would pour [sic] through 3+ years of tweets, cherry pick the weird/disturbing ones and use those to try to paint a portrait about me."

In a follow-up e-mail, David said the photograph was taken just after New Year's. He had been with Maura and her high school friends at a house in Goshen, New Hampshire, for the night. It was the same house the police were so interested in when she disappeared. The perfect place to lay low.

SIXTY-TWO

The Bitter and the Sweet

My grandfather passed away a few days after Christmas. A week before he died, he got a visit from a detective in Alliance who was investigating allegations of rape dating back forty years. My grandfather didn't eat a bullet like I hoped he would. The cancer got him.

There's no real closure. This is an existential world, my friend.

As of this writing, Maura's disappearance is still unsolved. As hard as I tried, I didn't get my *Girl with the Dragon Tattoo* ending. No meeting Harriet Vanger. Not yet.

As I was finishing the book, it dawned on me that I had never spoken to the people who owned the Seasons Resort in Bartlett, New Hampshire, where Maura had tried to rent a condo the day she went missing. I tracked down one of the condo owers, Linda Salamone, at home. It was little more than a fact-checking call, but it led to another strange revelation. The condo Maura was interested in had two separate bedrooms. It was not a single rental. It was a rental designed for families or groups of friends.

Fred and Maura used to stay together at the Seasons Resort when they traveled into the White Mountains.

When Salamone was contacted by police detectives years ago, one of them told her that the case "had taken a turn" and they didn't believe they needed the information she might have. The investigation, he said, was "going in another direction."

As I've said, Maura's case is a unique double mystery: 1) What happened to her? and 2) Why was she in New Hampshire to begin with? I believe I've answered the second question. It's obvious that Maura was running away. She had packed her belongings into boxes and left a message for her boyfriend. She'd returned her scrubs and bought herself a little time with professors by telling them that there had been a death in the family. She was never coming back. Maura was running away from her life and her family. I believe she thought that her credit card fraud and the identity theft associated with it were about to bury her. The charge would stick since she was going to be cited for the late-night accident in her father's car. She would never be able to pass the background checks required to become a nurse. It was time to start over.

But after that? What happened after the crash in New Hampshire?

After that, the best I can do is consider probabilities. The most likely explanation, the one that jibes with all the evidence, is that she was driving in tandem with someone who was aiding her escape. But who? Kate? Fred? I think the plan was for her to stay in New Hampshire for the night, perhaps so that her accomplice had time to travel up from Eastern Mass and meet her in the middle, on the Kancamagus Highway, and for them to travel into Canada in the morning. That other person could have been bringing her passport and other essentials from home. I think Maura made it to the rendezvous point (a restaurant, a gas station, a Dunkins) and was traveling behind her companion—or companions—when she got into her accident. The other driver doubled back, picked her up, and they continued on their way. Maura never expected that her disappearance would become national news, that her vanishing act would look so much like an abduction to some.

Do Maura's friends and family know where she is? I don't know. But I am at a loss to explain their behavior. They do not want this book written. It is clear to me that they are no longer actively looking for Maura. A reader on the blog summed it up well:

"To share a minor scare I had with one of my twins: When they were about three years old and just able to make their own choices, one of my girls wanted to go out in the back yard and get into the kiddie pool, but I told her to wait about ten minutes. The next thing I know she had disappeared. I looked everywhere in the yard.... Everywhere. I started to lose my mind. I ran screaming through the house, woke my wife up to help look. She searched through the house again and I jumped in our car and sped through the neighborhood screaming out of the window and praying out loud. I was in a total panic that I can't relate to anyone unless they have kids. When I got back to the house my wife was in the front yard with our missing daughter. She said that she basically reappeared when she was running through the house looking for her. I could feel my heart pounding in my chest and can never imagine being calm with a missing child. I would stop at nothing, sleeping only when necessary and never give up.

That small incident was too much for me. Even retelling it is upsetting. I guess everyone is different but these peeps have always behaved very oddly, IMHO."

Perhaps Maura is still in southern New Hampshire, working off the grid. There are plenty of folks around Haverhill doing that very thing.

I hope Maura ran away. I hope she found happiness elsewhere.

How do the rest of us go on without erasing our past mistakes and starting a new life? In a world of Ariel Castros and Amy Mihaljevics, how do we manage to move forward?

I think the secret may be that, in order to maintain our sanity, we need to find a way to ignore the constant threat of violence. That's not ignorance. No. I'm talking about a deliberate effort to turn our backs on bad news and to believe in grace, in eucatastrophe. To hope, even if you know better.

My wife said to me a couple weeks ago that I had lost my sense of joy, that I never smiled anymore. It was a profound statement. I still consider myself a funny guy. When we met in school, I was the class clown. Teachers were always saying I smiled too much. I was the joker. These stories, these adventures into the darker side of human nature, stole that away, like a dementor's kiss. I want to find my joy again.

My kids bring me joy. Casey and Lainey.

We have a wide backyard that looks into the woods that lead to the Cuyahoga. I keep the fence down in the back so the deer can sneak up to my house in the summers and nibble at the hostas. They're bedding back there now, keeping warm for the winter. Casey spotted a buck the other day, out the back door.

"Some people, they kill deer," he said. "They shoot them. I

would never kill an animal. They're so pretty, Dad. Aren't they? Why would anyone want to kill?"

"I don't know," I said.

Thus, I give up the spear.

EPILOGUE

There is no ending. Until there is.

One day, I will be sitting at a kid's gymnastics meet, or at lunch, or in front of the TV, and I'll check my smart phone and Maura Murray will be a trending topic on Twitter and Reddit. She will have come out of hiding to tell her story. Or maybe some hunter will have finally found her remains off a trail below Mount Washington. Until that day, the mystery is fluid. A book is a static thing. Unchanging. But a mystery moves. It lives. It evolves. Even as we edited this book, it evolved. At the eleventh hour, I discovered new information about Bill Rausch that caused me to question his role in the case.

Bill, I thought, was above suspicion—stationed at Fort Sill, in Oklahoma at the time of Maura's disappearance—and, I had come to believe, one of the good things in Maura's life. Just a few weeks ago, I gave an interview and said, "Maura was her best when she was with Bill." Now this was thrown into question.

On October 1, 2015, I received the following e-mail from "Ellen"*: "I prefer not to get involved but this case has been on my mind for a few years. It may be of interest to look further into Bill Rausch's character by way of employment history, relationships with co-workers, and reason for employment changes."

Later, she wrote: "I'd start at looking at LinkedIn and making connections—2010/2011."

I looked at Bill's employment history, again. In 2011, Bill Rausch was a director at Ray Group International, in D.C. He managed contracts in excess of $27 million and worked with Veterans Affairs and the Department of Defense, according to his LinkedIn profile. He left in May, 2011.

"What happened at Ray Group International?" I wrote back.

Ellen gave me the name of two coworkers, Margo and Sharon. Margo was the first one to tell me their story.

"This happened in March, 2011," she said over the phone, later that night. Margo, Carrie, and a third woman, Andie, had gone out for drinks after work to celebrate St. Patty's Day. Afterward, around 10 P.M., Andie needed to return to the office for some things, but by then the building was closed and locked up for the night. Luckily, Carrie had a key.

Carrie and Andie went in but when Carrie came out, Andie was nowhere to be found. Carrie went back in to find her. Margo got impatient waiting for them and crossed the street to go home. She looked back, though, and saw Andie come out of the building with Carrie. Andie looked upset. Margo texted Carrie: *What's going on with Andie?*

Carrie texted back that Bill Rausch had attacked her.

---

* names have been changed to protect sources

"When I went back in after Andie, the office was completely dark," Carrie explained. "I called out for her. She didn't respond. Then the big wooden doors to the president's office rattled, hard. Like someone trying to get out. Andie burst out and told me Bill had attacked her and was hiding under the president's desk."

Eventually, I spoke directly to Andie.

"Bill was strange around women," she began. "He was so arrogant and he had been making inappropriate comments to me and the other women. I assumed he didn't like me."

According to Andie, she had an odd encounter with Bill outside the subway one day a few weeks before the attack. She was coming up the elevators at the Metro on her way to work when Bill came up behind her and shoved her, hard, she said. She fell down. When she got to the office, she asked him about it. Why did he do it? But Bill acted like it wasn't him.

The night she came back to the office, after hours, Andie ran into Bill, who was married at the time. "He was clearly intoxicated. He said, 'I want to talk to you about something,' and then led me into the president's office and locked the door behind us." Once they were alone, according to Andie, Bill turned to her and smiled in a way that scared her. He said he knew that it was her he pushed in the Metro. She tried to leave. But Andie says he used his body to block her. He pushed her toward a wide table. Then, she said, he turned her around and pushed her facedown into the tabletop. She struggled. He pushed her down harder, she said.

At that moment, Carrie came back into the office, looking for Andie. They could hear Carrie outside the door. Andie said that Bill let her go at this time. "He said, 'Don't say a fucking word.'" Frightened for her life, Andie called out to Carrie. Bill made a "shushing" gesture to Andie, she said, and then hid his body under the president's desk. They got the door open and Andie left with Carrie.

Two days later, Andie said she went to the police station to fill out a report but ultimately decided not to.

"She was afraid of repercussions from Bill and, in my view, young and worried about the implications to her career," said Ellen.

But Andie did take it to the president of Ray Group International. Her coworkers backed her up. Bill never returned to the office and left to work at another company a month later.

Margo provided me with texts between her and Carrie from the day they spoke to the president of Ray Group International about Bill. Here's some of what they said:

Margo: *I basically told them that I don't feel safe, that Bill scares the crap out of me. I'm not the only one who feels this way and that Mike (the president) has no idea what Bill is actually like. I explained some of his erratic behavior in the past . . . I need to go for a walk but I basically aired out Bill's dirty laundry re: he's fucking crazy and a sociopath and doesn't understand human emotion.*"

Most of Bill's coworkers did not know that he was promised to marry Maura Murray. But Ellen says he once talked about her during a trip when he got to drinking one night. "He mentioned that they were in the midst of breaking up an engagement when she disappeared and, in retrospect, was glad that it worked out the way it did, which I took to mean how his life turned out, new marriage, etc."

"None of this behavior was shocking to me," said Margo. "This wasn't out of character. He had two personalities. One that he showed when he was only around women and one when he had to be around the men. We had a name for each personality. We called the mean one 'Bill' and the happy-friendly personality, 'Billiam.' I never wanted to interact with him. It was like, I don't know who you are but this is really weird."

I spoke to his direct assistant, Melissa, too. "Bill and I shared an office," she said. "At times, Bill became very erratic. He'd get very agitated sometimes. It was clear he didn't like any woman with authority. He was very territorial. Very possessive."

Melissa recalled when they were asked to travel to Ohio, where Bill's parents lived, on a project for the V.A. She thought Bill would be excited to go home but he said he didn't want to go. "I thought that was kind of odd."

"He had a really crazy reaction when he learned I was pregnant," said Melissa. He said he was happy for her, but the way he said it made Melissa uncomfortable. "You could tell he didn't mean it. It was very awkward." She'd brought sonogram pictures of the baby to show off to coworkers. She left them at her desk, in the office she shared with Bill, where he sat directly behind her. But when she returned later, they were gone. And she never found them again.

Finally, I spoke to Bill and asked him about Andie and Ray Group International. At first he denied knowing Andie. But after a couple minutes he said he did know her but was taken off guard by my questions. He wouldn't speak to the allegations and said he left Ray Group International for another job.

I think back on what others told me about Bill's relationship with Maura and see it in a new light.

Friends of Maura's from UMass said that Bill was very possessive of her and they tried to break them up, unsuccessfully. One man who did get close to Maura for a time, Hossein Baghdadi, was concerned about their relationship, calling Bill "controlling."

A reader of the blog recently found an old article about the case that had fallen off the Internet. In the article, Bill's mother, Sharon, said that her son was the "prime suspect" early in the investigation and recalled talking to him after being questioned. "He said, 'I feel as dirty as Scott Peterson. They think I've got something to do with it.'" Of course, I do know that the police will always immediately look at a boyfriend or husband as a suspect in a woman's disappearance.

I think about that e-mail Maura left on top of the boxes in her empty room, the e-mail that talked about Bill cheating on her. And I think about what former lead detective John Scarinza told me, about how he believed Maura might have just learned she was pregnant when she disappeared. I think about the House of Ruth, that beautiful underground railroad for abused women seeking a new life. And then I think about Bill's sister, Heather—who wanted to tell the sheriff about something illegal, according to the coroner.

Fort Sill is a twenty-six-hour drive from Haverhill, New Hampshire. It's nearly impossible to imagine that anyone could make a manic round-trip drive to New Hampshire and not be noticed, especially an officer in the Army. Still, I asked Bill what he was doing at Fort Sill in the days leading up to February 9, 2004. Bill says he was with Charlie Battery, and was "in the field" helping with basic training. "I was out of cell phone range," he said. He provided me with the names of two people who could verify that he was on base the whole time. I contacted both of these men. Neither called me back. Perhaps they just don't see the point of talking to me about a day in 2004 about which they have little, if any, recollection.

A few weeks after this revelation, I managed to get my hands on the call logs from both Bill and Maura's cell phones in the month leading up to her disappearance in 2004. After reviewing this information, I am confident that Bill, in fact, was at Fort Sill as he says he was. The records show that Bill was constantly calling offices around Fort Sill as part of his duties there. And at the time of Maura's accident in New Hampshire, Bill was making calls— which means he was nowhere near the White Mountains, where there is no cell service to this day. But—of course—the records reveal some strange things.

The night Maura had the breakdown at work, during a snowstorm that shut down the university, she placed a call to Domino's at 3:40 A.M. that lasted a couple minutes. This call is weird for several reasons. One, this is one of the restaurants where she used stolen credit cards to order food—why on earth would she ever call them again? Two, every source I've talked to says Domino's closed at 3 A.M. on Thursday nights. But maybe it's nothing.

More interesting are the calls placed by Bill. The day Maura vanished, the logs show that he was desperately trying to reach her throughout the day. He called her cell phone constantly but she never answered. He called Kate Markopoulos several times that day, too. At the moment Maura crashed into a snowdrift in New Hampshire, Bill was on the phone with a West Point professor— Bob McDonald—who used to host Bill and Maura at his house on occasion when they were cadets. Following this call, Bill made a flurry of phone calls to young women he knew in Ohio. I called them, too. "He was calling old girlfriends," one of them told me. When I told her about the alleged assault at Ray Group International, she said, "I'm not surprised to hear this."

Roaming charges show how Bill traveled to New Hampshire after Maura went missing, to help search for her, traveling to Vermont and Maine along the highways. He continued to try to reach Maura on her cell phone until the end of the billing cycle, in late February. He also continued to call Kate Markopoulos, but the length of these calls—usually under a minute—suggests he never reached her and she never called back. The calls to Kate Markopoulos stop after Bill called Sara Alfieri's phone number on February 19. What he learned from Sara that day remains a mystery.

Things that I've learned about Bill these last few months suggest that Maura could have had a good reason to flee. And if she really was pregnant, as Lt. Scarinza believes, a child gives her motive to remain hidden, when custody and visitation could be an issue.

If that is the case, then I hope Maura Murray remains missing.

ACKNOWLEDGMENTS

I should thank the stripper who inspired me to push on with my reporting, whose real name is neither Gracie nor Jennifer.

Karen Mayotte was my first major interview, and she provided great insight into the beginning of this mystery.

Without the inside information provided by Lieutenant John Scarinza and private investigators John Healy and Tom Shamshak, my job would have been much more difficult.

Thank you to the begrudging but welcoming community surrounding the site of Maura's accident in Haverhill, most notably Faith Westman and John Marrotte. I'm sorry for helping to make your little stretch of quiet New Hampshire so popular.

If my fiction editor, Sarah Crichton, had not taken a chance on my writing by shepherding *The Man from Primrose Lane*, I would never have been able to find the time and resources to devote to the adventures contained in this book.

A special thanks to my readers: Brandy Marks, Maggie

Antone, and Alyssa Carter, who proofread an early version of this book and provided very helpful notes about how to make it better.

My agent, Yishai Seidman, showed me how to find the better, leaner story within the manuscript.

My editor at Thomas Dunne Books, Nicole Sohl, took a chance on me and this story, and has my gratitude.

I also wish to thank Katie Bacon, Liz and Beth Drewniak, Mike Driscoll, Keith Erwin, Mike Lewis, Jeffery Strelzin, Ed Lanpher, John Green, Gnomini and the rest of my Irregulars, Cecil Smith, Dick Guy, Janis Mehrman, Kurt Noble, Tim Carpenter, Rick Graves, Nastaran Shams, Bill Rausch, Hossein Baghdadi, Crystal Therrien, Mike Lavoie, Chris King, Todd Landry, James Caccavaro, Dan Marks, Lorina Vasi, John Philpin, Dr. William Lee, Roger Synenberg, Dominic Coletta, Psychic Jean, Megan Sawyer, Barb Bressler, Joline Renner, Barbara Atwood, Lance Reenstierna, Tim Pilleri, Josh Leonard, David Whalen, Peter Hyatt, Jess Hicks, John B., Tyler from Pittsburgh, and Linda Salamone.

Anyone with information related to this case should contact the police directly at coldcaseunit@dos.nh.gov.